Fly with the Mourning Dove

Velda Brotherton

PublishAmerica
Baltimore

© 2007 by Velda Brotherton.

First printing

ISBN: 1-4241-5904-0
PUBLISHED BY PUBLISHAMERICA, LLLP
www.publishamerica.com
Baltimore

Printed in the United States of America

For Edna Smith Hiller, a tough westerner, whose love of the New Mexico high desert country inspired me to write this book. This is the true story of her life, as much as we could make it so. The people who lived, worked and played in the sage brush flats along the banks of the Rio Grande are real as she recreated them for me. Thanks, Edna, for sharing.

Prologue

In this, my ninetieth year, I've returned once again to the New Mexico ranch I'll forever call home. To this day, I get a thrill out of topping the hill between the sagebrush flats and the Tusas River valley. In the early light of dawn, the adobe house waits in the shadows far below, and I hurry to reach it, the car's tires clattering over the wooden bridge that spans the Tusas River. I park, get out and move through the yard. Over the Sangre de Cristos, the sky is splashed with a brilliant glow that spreads crimson across the mountains. In my valley the darkness retreats, stirs a breeze that touches my cheek.

If I turn from the rising sun, quickly and without warning, I see those who've left me behind—Mom and Pop, my one and only love Calvin and our precious Ann. The shimmering morning light offers them, real and alive, their laughter echoing across the San Juans far to the west, a high desert painting where shades of ochre contrast sharply with dense umbers.

The mournful song of the doves and the chatter of swallows swooping in to deposit small dabs of mud beneath the eaves of the stucco house, speak of another time. A time when my world was young and filled with hope.

Every spring I come home to cook my breakfast on the wood cookstove and eat on the porch and watch the elk drink from the snow melt of the river, drawn back year after year by forever memories, leaving behind that little tin can of a trailer down in Espanola for sanctuary at the only place I've ever called home. It is now a deserted ranch where no one but ghosts live, where cattle graze the high pastures, raising their heads to glimpse spirit riders as they pass.

The sun climbs higher, the sloping porch roof casts a cool shadow that makes me hug myself and shiver. I breathe in the fragrance of desert air, spiced with pinon smoke from the cookstove and the spring blooming chamisa, the sage and blue-balled juniper. And remember the beginning.

Chapter One

Cassie's Journal—1920

At times I wonder if it does a woman any good to have dreams. All my life I've wanted to be a nurse, and now that I finally have that chance, Finas tells me we are going to Taos County, New Mexico, to homestead 640 acres. What can sagebrush desert possibly have to offer?

First it was Montana, and living with our baby over a drugstore while he built us a house on that homestead. I know I married a cowboy, but I couldn't take the loneliness, scared half out of my mind over the idea of living in that wilderness.

In the end none of that matters. He's home from the war, I'm a nurse, and we are going to New Mexico.

We leave tomorrow and I'm going to hate it, I know. This time, though, I have to do what is right for Finas. For him and our child. Our family.

The train car swayed and clacked, wheels screeching against the narrow gauge rails that curved from Alamosa to Santa Fe. Chilled by the brisk November air, Cassie gathered her coat close and peered through her glasses at her husband.

"Tell me again why we're homesteading land in New Mexico," she said.

Finas turned those solemn brown eyes in her direction, and she experienced the same soul-stirring as she had the night they'd met. Because they couldn't bear to part, they'd taken so long walking home the short two blocks from the dance in the brittle North Dakota cold, that she'd literally frozen her nose.

"It won't be the same as Montana, I promise. I know you were lonely and scared when I dragged you and little Edna off to the ends of nowhere. This won't be the same."

She nodded, unsure of what to say. True, he had soon seen her misery and abandoned his plans of homesteading the Montana land to take a job in Minneapolis with Western Union. She loved him for that. But love was indeed a strange condition, and sometimes she resented that it bound her so tightly to this man.

The train lurched, throwing her against him. Six-year-old Edna stirred in her lap, but continued to sleep. For a moment, Cassie kept her head against his shoulder. He cupped the side of her face, his palm warm against her cheek.

"Cassie, I'm sorry."

She twisted to look into his eyes, sunken in the pale face. Dark circles smudged his cheeks, and she felt shame.

"It's not your fault. But I just wonder if there isn't fresh air and sunshine in Casselton or some other civilized town."

When the doctors in Salt Lake City had diagnosed him with tuberculosis she'd felt her heart shrivel in her chest. This healthy, robust man surely couldn't be so ill.

He stiffened against her. "Your parents don't like me, Cassie. We'd soon be miserable."

She translated that as he'd be miserable, but he spoke the truth.

Her mother and sisters had whispered and tut-tutted about poor Cassie falling for such a man as he. A cowboy, for goodness sake. And from Kentucky? Whoever heard of such a thing? But that's what he was, through and through. A cowboy and a southern gentleman. And despite their differences she had fallen hard the minute she laid eyes on him. And she loved him dearly, even though he strode through life sweeping aside all barriers while ignoring the consequences.

"We'll make a home for ourselves out here and I'll get well. Besides, look how close we'll be to the sun. Seven thousand feet high, honey. Think of it. That ought to do a lot of good. And you can't find better air than the high desert."

Regrettably, she was thinking of it, staring out the coaldust-streaked window at the sagebrush stretching for mile upon mile. To the east the Sangre de Cristos cut into a brilliant sky, to the west the less magnificent San Juans. Fencing in the clean, clear air and empty, lonely spaces. She would go crazy out here.

"It just seems a bit rash, that's all." Her frown chased away his smile. For that she was sorry, but couldn't seem to bring herself to apologize.

They'd boarded the narrow gauge known as the Chili Railroad at Alamosa, Colorado, and since leaving the broad green valley and Antonito, the steam engine had chugged upward through sagebrush flats. The black smoke from its stack deposited grit on her clothes and between her teeth.

She caught him studying her, eyes again bright and hopeful. How he wanted her to accept this place he had chosen for them. How terribly afraid she was that she would hate it, that it would be like his ranch in Montana. Remote, terrifying, cold and isolated from humanity.

"Tell me again about our new home," she said.

Clasping her hand, he gazed out the window, deep in thought, trying to get the words right to convince her everything would be okay, that she would learn to like this alien land.

"At Taos Junction we'll have a wagon ride, but it won't be too far." He glanced at her to see how she was taking his words. "M.B. will meet us there, and our place is only about five miles to the north."

She gazed at the prickly gray brush stretching to the horizon. "And will it look like this? Our place?"

A coughing fit took hold and he hunched his shoulders against it, pawed a handkerchief from his coat pocket and covered his mouth. Then he curled his other hand over hers and waited until his breath came with regularity before speaking.

"The land is fertile and crops grow well. There's plenty of rain and snow. I'll make us a good home here."

A long pause dragged her gaze toward him. Both remembering other promises left behind to fade like dust. Surely he omitted those things she wouldn't like. "And this Taos Junction place. Is there...are there stores and the like?"

"Stong. That's what they call the post office." A nervous laugh told her more than the words. "And there is a general store as well, and a school."

Her heart might as well have thudded to a stop, for she could scarcely catch her breath. "And how many acres do we have?"

"Six hundred forty. That's how much we are allowed to homestead. M.B. has the same next to ours. We've built the houses, yours and Mae's, close together so you'll be neighbors. There aren't any other women..." He broke off, clearly aware this was not a selling point.

What was she doing here? What if she didn't like this Mae person? She tightened her grip in his, her small hand all but swallowed by his larger one. The open country frightened her small-town mentality. She had trouble envisioning spaces that weren't measured in blocks.

"Six hundred forty acres. That's a lot, isn't it?"

"It is, but it takes plenty of desert range to feed cattle. The grass is rich but sparse. The animals adapt."

"Cattle?" Something else she hadn't thought of.

His eyes glistened. "We're building a ranch, Cassie. Yes, cattle. And sheep and horses. You can have some chickens if you want, and we'll plant a garden, so you and Mae can put up vegetables for the winter months."

That frightened her even more. "I'm not much of a cook. You know that." Disturbed by the admission, she turned to meet his steady gaze. "But I am a good nurse, Finas. A good nurse. People need nurses." Though not in the middle of this godforsaken desert. A legitimate certainty she kept to herself.

"You're my wife and you're a nurse. I suppose folks around here may be grateful for the latter." His drawl tightened. He was growing impatient with her.

Yet, she couldn't help herself, and grumbled back at him. "And this land that they're giving veterans who've fought for their country…no one else wants it, else why would they give it away?"

"Now, Cassie, that's not exactly true. There've been homesteaders since the movement west. And most of them have done very well with the land."

"Well, I never heard of it, not in North Dakota, or anyplace else. It's 1920, for goodness sake, not 1850 or whatever."

"The Homestead Act was meant to lure settlers out west after the Civil War was over. And it's still intact." His words trailed off. "It was just a different war. New Mexico hasn't been a state very long. Eight years."

"Who will live around us? I'm afraid it might be riff-raff."

"Hardly. Most of these vets homesteading have some college behind them. They're looking for a fresh start after the war. A peaceful place. They are all good fellows. Most of them from Texas. Nothing to be frightened of."

She fingered Edna's curls, nestled the warmth of the sleeping child against her breast, envisioned wild cowboys.

"Tell me about the house." Her voice sounded strained, but she didn't mean it to.

The tuberculosis ravaging his lungs was an enemy lurking in the darkest shadows, ready to pounce…ready to ruin everything. She did so want him to get well, to be happy. But fear of where they were going clutched her heart in its fist and she found no way to defeat it. She had a vague feeling that he welcomed this chance, this disease that forced them to leave the city and head once more for the desolation of ranch life. Of course, that was ridiculous.

"Right now it's three rooms, honey. And it's not much, but once we get settled in, I'll do some more work on it."

"Three rooms," she echoed.

"One big room, two little ones. There are windows. Honey, we don't have much to start with. It's just a tar-paper affair for now, built of one-by-twos and two-by-fours."

Imagining what he described brought fresh tears to her eyes. She thought of her family's large, sprawling home on Cooney's Island in

Casselton. The laughter of her sisters as they chased one another through the rooms and out across the lush lawn. Staring at the brown sagebrush, she yearned for green trees and the thick, sweet grass of North Dakota.

Where was the grass here, for goodness sake? And the water?

"Mom," Edna murmured, stirred and tugged at her sleeve.

Grateful for the interruption, Cassie turned her attention to their daughter. "Yes, sweetheart."

"Mom, I'm hungry and cold."

"Crawl up here in my lap," Finas said in the tone he only used with his beloved daughter. "Your dad will keep you warm. And look here what I've got." He fished a paper wrapped cookie from his coat pocket.

Where on earth had he gotten that? How clever of him to anticipate the child's needs. Cassie touched his arm and smiled when he glanced down at her.

Edna did as her father bid and accepted the cookie shyly. This man called Dad was a stranger to her. First he was away at war, and then he no more than come home than she'd been hustled off to live in Kentucky with Grandma and Grandpa. Still, when he came to fetch her last week, she'd had a vague notion of missing him. Though not used to being with him yet, she welcomed his arms around her, the feel of his rough coat against her cheek, the special smell only he had. Living with Grandma and Grandpa had been fine, but she was happy to be with Mom…and Dad again.

Now they were going to live on a ranch. The three of them. Taking a last bite of the sweet cookie, she nestled deep into the folds of Dad's thick, wooly coat and fell asleep, dreaming of the ranch and a beautiful white horse that would be hers.

The loud rattle of moving wheels and a terrible shaking awoke Edna. For a moment, she didn't know where she was. She was no longer on the clackety train, but wrapped tightly and being jostled until her teeth chattered. Peering from the small gap in a cocoon of blankets, she saw it was almost dark. The sun painted orange streaks across the sky, so she could see Mom's face. Her scowly face, not the happy one. They were in a wagon pulled by horses. Two of them. The cold air nipped at her cheeks and she burrowed deeper in the warmth. Already she missed school and her room at Grandma and Grandpa's and the smell of wood smoke.

Here the air smelled like ice and snow, something spicy she couldn't place and the pleasant odor of horses.

Someone hollered "Whoa," and the wagon rolled to a stop.

"Down there," a voice she didn't know said. "I built you a fire before we left. It'll be cozy warm inside, Missus."

"Thanks, M.B.," Dad said.

Mom didn't say anything.

Excited, Edna struggled from under the folds of blanket to stare off across the flats at two small houses, mere shadows in the growing dusk. The golden glow of lamplight shone from one, the other was dark. And all around, as far as she could see, spiky bushes sprawled over the ground, like silent forms of strange animals frozen in flight. Her breath hung like clouds of fog around her head. Sagebrush, Dad had called it. Her heart tripped around in her chest. There was nothing out here. No one...nothing. No wonder Mom looked so scowly.

And where in the world would she go to school?

"There's no water. How can we live without water?"

These were the first words Edna heard when she awoke the next morning to brilliant sunshine streaming through the window onto her pallet.

"Now, darling. We'll haul in water. You'll have all you need." Daddy sounded unhappy.

"From where? Look out there. I don't see any water. And look at this place. A cookstove, table and chairs, shelves on the wall and one bed." By then Mom was pacing, her fat-heeled shoes thud-thudding on the wide floorboards.

"After the holidays I'm taking Edna back to Kentucky so she can go to school." Mom didn't sound any too happy.

"Now, Cassie. We can talk about it some more after we get used to the place. There's a school in Taos Junction. I want us all to be together. We've been apart too long."

Rising from the floor, Edna rubbed her eyes awake just in time to see Mom stride to the table where Dad sat drinking coffee and plant her hands on her hips. Bad sign.

"You call that a school? That little dump of a place? She can't learn anything there. She has to go back, at least till she finishes first grade."

Tears burned Edna's eyes but she blinked them away. Only sissies cried. "Mom, Dad—" She was going to say she wanted to stay here, but both turned and greeted her as if they hadn't been arguing. Putting on their happy faces.

"Good morning, sweetheart," Mom said. "Come have some breakfast." Her voice quavered.

"Did you sleep well?" Dad asked. "After you eat I'll take you around to look at the place. There's not much here yet, but I can show you where we'll build the barn for the horses."

Mom glared from Dad to Edna and back at Dad. "I suppose you'll do what you please." She went to the window, squeezing her shoulders tight together so her pretty flowered dress bunched up around the back of her neck.

Edna felt sorry for Mom. But horses. Dad had said horses.

He knew how much she wanted a horse. It had been one of the first things she told him when he came to Kentucky to get her, when he said they were going to have a ranch in New Mexico. But looking around the small house, she felt sad. This didn't look like a ranch to her. Not in the least. And she couldn't much blame Mom for being upset.

Even so, she hurried to eat her oatmeal, get dressed and slip into her coat. When they were ready to leave, Dad asked Mom to come along, but she said no, she wanted to try to fix things up a bit. Edna wasn't sure what could be fixed up, but she was happy to be asked to go with Dad, and so didn't worry too much about it. If Mom could fix things up, then everything would probably be all right.

On the porch, Dad hefted a saddle to one shoulder and led her across the yard where he whistled up a pretty dun horse. Her stomach rolled over and her heart skipped around till she could hardly contain herself. She and Dad were going to ride this beautiful horse. The dun tossed its head and snorted white mist into the crisp air, stretching its neck to sniff at her. Cupping one hand she rubbed the velvety nose, then leaned forward and kissed it. He smelled wonderful, like wet earth and grass.

No matter what Mom said or did, she would stay here. She would ride over their ranch with Dad, helping him with whatever it was one did on a ranch.

"Come on, sweetheart," he said, and reached out to her.

She grabbed hold of his big, broad hand, and he swung her up in the saddle, then mounted behind her. Ever so easy, he touched the dun's sides with his boot heels. They were moving…galloping out through the sagebrush, the cold wind in her face and hair. It was the most magical moment in her life, and she vowed never to forget it.

Chapter Two

Cassie's Journal—1920

Mae and I are the only white women living here. In Taos Junction are the Patchen and Wilton families, and that is it.

It is dry, so dry. They say dryer than it has been in years. We spend all our money on crops and improvements.

It is especially lonely for Edna. There are no children for miles. The Patchens have all gone off to school. Edna only went to school a few months in Clay, Kentucky, and I'm seriously thinking of taking her back down there after the holidays. Finas may be upset with me, but she is not the only one who is lonely. I yearn for green grass and an early morning mist that leaves teardrops on flowers and leaves.

Cassie would have kicked the oven door, or at the least, tossed the ruined cake against the wall, if she hadn't been raised in a refined Victorian household. As it was, she banged the pan of ruined batter onto the table and paced the room several times before stopping to stare out the window. Pellets of snow raced sideways, blurring the mountains into indistinct humps.

A wagon rattled into the yard.

Finas and Gus, home with water, just in time for her to clean up the mess she'd made. Feet stomped across the porch and the door swung open.

"Cassie, you here?"

Mae Marr. "Where else? Come in. I thought you were Finas and Gus. They went to Taos Junction after water."

"It is. I mean they are. I hitched a ride over. Didn't feel up to walking in this storm." Mae unwrapped a long woolen muffler from her head and shed her coat, then stood by the stove shivering. "The men are unhitching the team."

Without taking off her gloves she helped herself to coffee from the percolator on the cook stove. Both hands wrapped around the cup, she took a long sip.

"Ah, that's better. Smells…uh, odd in here."

All Cassie could produce was a wry grin. "Ruined another cake. I don't suppose I'll ever learn to bake at this altitude. Truth is, I never was much good at creating delectable goodies in Casselton either."

Mae laughed with a heartiness typical of her breeding. Raised in Milwaukee, she was often outspoken, always gregarious. Like Cassie, she had not adapted well to conditions on the homestead, but was determined to make the best of it. Neither had much of a choice.

"Yummy, sounds good. Cut me a piece."

Together, they sat at the table and eyed the pan and its flattened contents.

After a long moment of contemplation, Mae glanced up. "Well, I think I'll pass."

"I tested the oven temperature with a piece of wrapping paper, too. It only curled, didn't scorch. What could we be doing wrong?"

"Not we, I gave up. It's cobblers or nothing around our house."

Cassie poured herself a cup of tea from the steeping pot and stirred it listlessly. "Whatever brings you out on a day like this?"

"Was sort of hoping you wouldn't ask, then I could say I forgot to tell you." Glancing around, she asked, "Where's that darling child?"

"Taking a nap. Mae, stop stalling. What's up? Give."

"I knew that wouldn't work. Okay, here goes. It seems you and I have been drafted to cook the turkey for Thanksgiving dinner at the Patchens' house next week."

Hand spread wide over her chest, Cassie stared at Mae, whose fashionable bob remained plastered to her head. "Turkey? Us? You and me? Whose bright idea was that? I've never even cleaned a chicken, much less a bird as big as…" She narrowed her eyes. "Just how big is this turkey?"

"Haven't seen it, don't know. It's still running around in a pen in their back yard. Ditto on that chicken thing. Ben knows better than to bring anything in the house with its head or innards intact."

"It's alive?" Cassie choked on a swallow of tea. "Well, you can just tell them no. Or better yet, tell them I'm confined to my sick bed. I'll be down at least till after Christmas in case they have any ideas about me killing and butchering a hog for the ham. Tell them. I'm having nothing to do with killing or cooking a running-around, covered-with-feathers bird." She stared into her cup. "And it looking at me with big, sad, pleading eyes. Oh, not me. Huh-uh."

"Oh, no, you don't. If I'm in this, you are too."

"What if we both were sick? I'm a nurse, I can come up with some terrific symptoms. Like typhoid fever...or better yet, something fatal. Take me completely away from all of—"

Before Cassie could finish, Finas and Gus stomped their feet outside and burst through the door.

"You ladies get your problems solved? Gus here is ready to git on home. He can take you, Mae."

"Fine, thanks." Mae glared at Cassie. "We'll have to be there really early, Cassie, to get that bird in the oven."

"Mae," Cassie warned, but could think of nothing else. Not with Finas gazing at her with those adoring brown eyes. He had something to do with this, and she could cheerfully smack him one.

"Oh, hon, I forgot to tell you we'd been invited to eat Thanksgiving dinner with the Patchens, and I thought seeing as how you've had so much trouble with the stove and all, it'd be a relief to you, so I said yes. Is that what you two were talking about?"

"Yes, my darling, that's what we're talking about."

With a final, steely glance at Cassie, Mae wrapped her head, slipped into the heavy coat and hurried to the door. "Ready anytime you are," she said and slithered out ahead of Gus, fingers wiggling good bye.

"You'd better run," Cassie muttered.

"What?" Finas said.

"If I were you, I wouldn't bring it up."

He stared into his cup of coffee, unable to hide a grin.

Finas decided they should drive in to the Patchens' house the evening before Thanksgiving. "Weather isn't looking so good. Gus will feed and water the stock for us. Says he wants no part of such a gathering, and you know him."

Cassie kept her lips tight to shut off words it would be wisest not to utter, while Finas continued to rattle on as if this dinner were the biggest event to ever hit Taos Junction. It probably was, but Cassie couldn't get too excited. Visions of a big, strutting, fully-feathered bird waiting to be killed so she could render it naked and...she couldn't even imagine what came next.

"Now, don't you worry a bit about that bird. I already said I would wring its neck and scald off the feathers. All you'll have to do is stick it in the oven."

She glared in his direction. "Don't forget I have to de-gut the thing."

He sipped coffee and kept silent. If she ever found out he had anything to do with volunteering her for this job, he'd regret it. For a long time. She shuddered at the thought of putting her hands inside the dead bird.

While she helped Edna bundle up for the drive to Taos Junction, he kept right on talking. And she knew why he chattered on, too. It was to keep her from blowing up about the entire situation.

"Old Lady Patchen promised us a bed. Said there isn't much business in the boarding house this time of the year. Guess travelers stay home for the holidays." Finas laughed. "Said, since you and Mae were so kind as to volunteer your services, she wouldn't charge us for overnight."

"Swell of her. Volunteer, indeed." Glowering, she buttoned Edna's coat, wrapped a quilt around her and picked her up. "If you're ready, I am."

"The wagon awaits, my lady," he said, pulled on his coat and hat and swung open the door. "I'll carry the baby."

"I'm not a baby," Edna protested from out of the folds.

"Of course you're not," Cassie said, and glared at Finas. "I can carry her just fine, thank you."

"Well, then, let's go."

Finas entered the hot kitchen through the back door accompanied by a gust of icy wind and a very dead, very naked bird. One huge hand clasping scaly clawed feet, he swung it onto the counter where it landed with a dull thump.

"Right here's where you cut him open." His finger slashed downward between the legs. "Pull out the guts." With a flash of his wicked grin he beat a quick retreat.

"You'd better run, you traitor."

"Did you say something?" Mae came out of the pantry, tying on an apron and eyeing the bird with revulsion.

"Finas, you coward. You come back here. What do I do about these?" Cassie pointed at one long disgusting toenail encrusted with something unmentionable. Her shout bounced off his hunched shoulders, but didn't slow him down.

With a sigh she patted the still warm breast and raised an eyebrow at Mae, who appeared white as the flesh of the recently deceased turkey.

"Do something. You're the nurse."

"Well, at least it smells dead." Cassie peered through her glasses at the huge breast. Here and there a feather clung tenaciously to the pale skin that appeared to have permanent goose bumps.

"It is dead," Mae muttered.

The lump in Cassie's throat grew to enormous proportions till she couldn't speak.

Okay. Just do this. What could be so bad? She'd lanced boils, cleaned and dressed bleeding and infected wounds, mopped up vomit. Surely to goodness she could clean this poor dead fowl. At least it couldn't object.

The Old Hickory butcher's knife Mrs. Patchen had left on the counter looked as deadly as a scalpel. She gripped the handle, gnawed her lower lip and pricked at the skin, fully expecting the thing to caw or gobble or something. It just lay there.

Mae remained inert as a corpse, hands clasped over her mouth.

Well, she wouldn't get away with that. "Grab his legs," she ordered.

Eyes going wider, Mae shook her head.

"Mae, we're in this together. Now get hold of yourself. I mean, him."

"I don't think I can."

Cassie waved the knife like a weapon. "Of course you can."

Cocking a wary eye at the long blade, Mae shuffled forward. "Okay, here I come." Keeping her distance, she leaned out and wrapped the fingers of one hand around an inert foot. A gurgle escaped from her throat.

"Mae, for goodness sake. Get hold of his legs."

"What are you going to do?"

"Eviscerate him."

"Oh." Mae let go, swallowed hard and gagged.

"Don't you dare. Now get a good hold and spread 'em wide."

Tears welled in Mae's eyes. "It wouldn't be so hard if he'd cut off the feet. They look so…so…nasty. Maybe we could get him to come back and chop off the feet?"

"He comes back in here, I'm liable to chop off something for him. Now just catch hold. Do it."

"Okay, okay. I've got him."

And she did, more or less, by standing two feet away, bent at the waist, clasping the skinny legs so tight her knuckles whitened.

Tucking her lips firmly between her teeth, Cassie pressed the point of the knife into the flesh, shuddered as a great gash ripped open. A warm, fetid smell made her gag. "That is disgusting."

"Stick your hands inside and pull out everything."

"I'm not putting my hands inside there."

Mae spread the legs wider, shuffled closer and took a look. "Well, I'm not either."

Cassie set her shoulders. "One of us has to." She knew without looking at Mae's expression, who that would be.

"Think of it as…shoot, I can't think of anything."

Mrs. Patchen bustled into the kitchen carrying a metal dishpan. "Just pull them innards out into here. And don't forget to save the neck and liver and heart and gizzard to cut up in the dressing. I need to get them started boiling. I'm just going to get it all mixed up before I set the bread to rise."

Cassie stared at the woman, who looked way too happy. Well, why not? She didn't have to gut a dead turkey. She dragged in a deep breath. The kitchen smelled of spicy pumpkin pies baked the night before. But over it all hung the horrible smell of hot, recently living innards. She wouldn't be able to eat a bite.

"Come on, child, we need that old fellow in the oven if we're going to eat today. Lord knows he'll need plenty of cooking. He's been around nearly as long as we have. Probably be a tough old thing, but we'll manage."

Even as the portly woman talked about the poor dead fowl, she deftly fetched a wooden bread bowl, opened the flour bin and measured several cups of flour.

Cassie glanced at Mae, and both eyed the gaping wound left by the sharp blade. No doubt about it, she had to reach inside there with her hands and pull out the entrails.

Mae elbowed her. "Go on, you can do it. Just pretend it's a patient."

"I've never gutted a patient."

"Well, you know what I mean."

Indeed she did, and delaying the inevitable only made it worse. Mama had always said that the more you thought of something unpleasant, the worse the task became. Of course, she had never so much as cleaned a chicken, let alone laid hands on a fowl as big as this guy. Servants did that sort of work. Coming in close contact with dead animals wasn't something Victorian ladies so much as considered. The entire family had a fit when Cassie entered nurse's training. The idea of touching dirty old men was beneath them. And Papa, well, he'd had a wall-eyed conniption fit to think of one of his girls performing such menial tasks.

What would they think now?

Mrs. Patchen's impatient glance made it clear she and Mae had wasted enough time. Cassie squinched her eyes shut, plunged one hand inside the bird and closed her fingers around the slimiest mess she'd ever encountered in her entire lifetime. Warm and wormy and gooey in there. Her stomach heaved and she bent forward. A handful of "guts" sucked loose and slithered into the pan. And if she'd thought the earlier stench bad, it was nothing compared to the one that accompanied the long, ropy blue cords.

Quicker done, quicker over. Breathing through her mouth, Cassie plunged her hand back inside and dragged out more innards.

"You save the liver and gizzard and heart now," Mrs. Patchen called, her voice so cheerful Cassie wanted to lasso her with a loopy intestine.

"Where are they?" Mae whispered.

"How should I know?"

"Some nurse you are."

"People don't have gizzards, how would I know where it is? Or even what it looks like. Now stop talking and hang on to the pan. Don't you dare dump that on the floor."

At last Mrs. Patchen stepped up to work loose the liver, heart and gizzard for her dressing. "You can just toss that out back." She gestured at the pan. "Carry it a ways from the house. I don't want the coyotes coming too close."

Cassie grabbed the pan and fled out the back door and down off the stoop, carrying the mass of turkey innards. She stumbled through drifts of snow, dodging sagebrush, lungs burning with each breath. Behind her, Mae ran to keep up, laughing heartily.

"Far enough, far enough," she called. "We go any farther we won't get back in time to stick that bird in the oven and get it cooked for dinner." Continued laughter disrupted the words.

Cassie stopped, turned and glared at her. "What are you laughing at?" An icy wind cut through her dress, and she gasped to catch her breath.

Hugging herself, Mae gained a semblance of control. "My God, did you ever see anything so funny? Me holding that poor turkey's legs wide while you dug into that mess. You ought to've seen your face. I thought you were a nurse. I thought you would've seen a lot worse. Blood and guts and the like."

Cassie tossed the writhing mess onto the ground and turned away. "Nothing I've ever seen, nothing, has been worse than this."

Mae shivered and jiggled to keep warm, eyes sparkling with mirth. "Well, maybe that's a good thing. You have to admit it was funny."

"I don't have to admit any such thing." Cassie took a last quick look at the coyote's supper, then shuddered. "At least it doesn't look so bad when it's frozen."

"If we don't get back inside, we'll be frozen too." Mae danced a circle, then broke into a run, Cassie on her heels, both hysterical with laughter.

The mood continued throughout the day. Each time Cassie caught Mae's eye she stuck out her tongue and rolled her eyes and they both broke into gales of laughter. Must have been the relief both felt that the worst was over.

At last, Finas carried the browned turkey to the table and sat it before Mr. Patchen for carving.

Edna, who had been scarcely able to contain herself surrounded by so much excitement and so many people, declared in a loud voice, "Daddy, I want the drumstick. That's the best part."

Once again laughing, Cassie bent down to her child. "Honey, wherever did you hear that?"

Edna shrugged and pinned her mother with wide eyes. "I don't know. Maybe Grandpa Smith?" She nodded, sure she was right. "That's the very best part of the turkey. Please, Mama. Please."

Taking up the large carving knife, Mr. Patchen sawed through the bird's leg, separated it from the thigh with some difficulty and lay it on a plate. "Here, then, little one. It's the drumstick you want, it's the drumstick you get."

"That's far too much for the child," Cassie said. "Why don't you just slice her off a little?"

"Nonsense," Mrs. Patchen said. "Let her have it."

Seated in the chair, her chin barely above the table top, Edna picked up the drumstick in both hands and gnawed away at it. Or at least, tried to. Tasted sort of good, but hard to tear off a bite. Harder yet to chew it.

She held the chunk of meat away from her mouth and squinted at it.

Mama laughed and so did Aunt Mae. Then everyone joined them.

Determined, she went at the leg again, twisting it this way and that to find the best point of attack. No matter how hard she tried, she couldn't chew the tough meat. It had long, white slivers of bone through it too. How could anyone think this was good?

Disappointment brought tears to her eyes, but she swiped them away with the backs of greasy hands.

"Use your napkin, Edna," Mama said. "Would you like some mashed potatoes to go with your drumstick?"

When she nodded, Mama grinned and gave her a spoonful, then proceeded to fill her plate from the bowls of food passed around the table.

Edna watched Mama cutting a slice of white meat on her own plate. "I think I would like to try a different piece of turkey."

"Oh, no, child, that will never do," said Mr. Patchen. "It's the drumstick you wanted, it's the drumstick you have."

Mama leaned down, whispered to her. "Never mind, dear. The rest of the turkey is every bit as tough as your drumstick." A giggle threatened, and Mama glanced around the table. "Actually not worth the work it took to cook it. Eat your vegetables and we'll have a nice piece of pumpkin pie."

"I think we should have ham for Thanksgiving next year, don't you?"

"I think that's a wonderful idea." Mama laughed and Aunt Mae did too. It really wasn't that funny, surely, but Edna joined in anyway.

She looked around the table at everyone talking and eating and having a good time. What a wonderful place this was. But she was afraid, for she'd heard Mama and Daddy talking again about her going back to Kentucky to finish school after the holidays. It wasn't that she didn't love Grandma and Grandpa. She did, with all her heart. But now that she'd lived with Mama and Daddy here in New Mexico, she couldn't bear the thought of parting from them. Or of leaving this place she loved so much.

They had a secret, a terrible secret and she found herself hoping she never learned what it was. Maybe if she crossed her fingers and wished really hard, they'd let her stay here on the ranch with them. And maybe their secret, whatever it was, would go away.

She smiled across the table at her new friends, and decided to give the tough drumstick one more try.

Chapter Three

I will be glad to leave the ranch to go after Edna. The lovely green of Kentucky will be a relief from this everlasting drab dull brown.

A nearby rancher, John Marcum, married a half-breed Indian woman who chews tobacco and acts crazy most of the time, but she's no company.

Still no rain, and not much snow last winter, either.

The government didn't give the boys the world by the tail. Instead they gave us these miserable arid homesteads and we not only have to put in several hundred dollars' worth of improvements, we must live long on it before it will be ours.

Is it worth it? I don't know.

Leaning her nose against the smudgy window Edna peered at the trees and rolling hills. They closed around her like a gigantic blanket. It would be so good to get back where the sagebrush flats reached out to forever and the endless blue sky dipped down to touch the distant mountaintops.

Mother looked sad, sitting straight beside her, eyes closed behind her glasses, hands clasped in her lap.

Unable to contain herself, Edna tugged at her sleeve. "I can't wait, I can't. Why must it take so long?"

"Don't be silly, of course you can wait." She paused, gazed out the window. "I will miss the green grass and trees, I surely will."

"I missed you and Daddy. I missed the mules and the sheep and going riding with Daddy."

Mother touched her knee. "Sit back, darling. Stop fidgeting. I know you missed everything and I'm so sorry. But we'll be home soon."

Edna managed to obey, but continued to chatter. "Now I suppose I will miss Grandma and Grandpa. But I won't miss this place because I'll be home with you and Daddy and Major and all the—"

"Darling, please. I have a headache." She took off her glasses and rubbed at her eyes.

Though sorry Mother didn't feel good, Edna twisted and turned, unable to remain in the seat. Under her feet wheels clacked and the car swayed. They passed through lush green pastures with white fences that hemmed in beautiful horses. Excited by the moaning of the train whistle, the animals ran and played, manes and tails flying, trying to keep up. She imagined sitting astride that big white one, racing flat out across the desert. The wind in her face would carry the sweet smell of blooming sage.

Beside her Mother returned her glasses to her nose and adjusted the earpieces, then stared straight ahead. She wouldn't even look at the beautiful animals, but twisted her fingers in her lap.

"Is Daddy waiting for us at the station?"

"He will be when we get there."

"How long will it be?

Mother shrugged, didn't answer.

"How are the horses?"

"Fine." This time she sighed.

"And the mules?"

"They're fine too."

"And the sheep and their—"

"Darling, please." A long, stern look.

"I just want to know."

Mother patted her hand so she knew everything was all right. Sometimes Mother was tired or vexed and acted mad, but Daddy never allowed it to last long. He would tease and hug her, and even though she pulled away and tried not to smile, he could always get her to. And she never, ever stayed angry very long.

Grandma and Grandpa didn't either, but sometimes, when she galloped through the house astraddle of Grandma's broom, Grandpa would go outside and sit on the porch.

Oh, goodness, they'd soon be home. Happiness danced inside her like sparkles off fireworks.

"Mother?"

"What?" No longer angry, maybe impatient, but that was all.

"I don't want to go away from you and Daddy again. I can go to school at home. They have a school there, and I promise I'll be really good so you won't have to send me away again."

Mother looked sad and touched Edna's cheek. "We didn't send you away because you weren't good. We wanted you to finish school where you began the year, that's all."

"So you won't send me away to school…ever again?"

Mother grew distant and took her hand away. "We'll see. I guess we'll see."

It seemed like they traveled forever. Once they changed trains but, half asleep, she didn't pay attention to where they were. All she could think of was getting home to the ranch and Daddy. When she slept lots of time went by, but she was much too excited to close her eyes for very long. It was dark when the conductor finally came down the aisle, swaying with the movement of the train so he had to catch hold of the backs of each seat.

"Tos Junction. All out for Tos Junction."

She giggled at the way he said Taos Junction, and hopped up and down. "Come on, Mother. Come on, we're home."

"Sit down, darling. Wait till the train stops. Sit down, now, child." Mother tugged at her sleeve, and Edna sank to the edge of the seat. She jumped up and down several times because she couldn't help herself, then sat when Mother scowled.

That didn't matter. Nothing did. They were home.

The next morning she awoke in her own bed, so excited she could hardly take time to remove her gown and put on her dress. Barefoot, she ran into the kitchen. The sun was barely up, its golden glow forming a halo around Mother, who stood at the stove stirring oatmeal.

"Wash your hands and face and eat some breakfast."

"Okay, where's Daddy?" She skirted the table, went to the door and threw it open, sniffed deeply of the smell of horses and pinon and desert. She leaned out to gaze around. Chains rattled near the new barn where Daddy and another man hitched two mules to the wagon. Three barrels sat in the bed. She scooted across the porch. Nothing had changed. Not the wind blowing off the snow tipped mountains, or the brilliant rays of sunlight painting the desert so pretty it like to made her cry.

"Edna, come back inside and put on your stockings and shoes. For goodness sake, child. Did your grandparents spoil you rotten? Have you forgotten your manners?"

"Where's Daddy going?"

"To Taos Junction after water."

"Can I go? Please, Mother, let me go with him."

"That's no job for a lady, child. Besides, he'll be gone all day. You'll stay here with me."

"If I asked him and he said okay?"

"No, I said no. You stay here and we'll make some clothes for the fairies. They have missed you terribly and are practically going naked."

"Oh, that's silly. Naked fairies?" The idea of fairies dancing in the woods without wearing a stitch made her giggle.

"Child, will you close the door and finish dressing this minute? And bring me a brush so I can fix your hair."

Edna fingered her straight locks as she went for her shoes and stockings and the brush. Her hair was the same color as Mother's but thick and straight. Mother had beautiful hair, dark and cut so the curls hugged her head all over.

In the months Edna had been in Kentucky, Grandma had not cut hers, and the short bob had grown till it almost reached her shoulders. Straight, not curly at all. Mother would cut it soon. Short for the hot summer days.

Aunt Mae arrived while Mother was fooling with her hair. Edna's stomach growled and she wished she could eat her breakfast, growing cold on the table, but Mother just kept brushing. Daddy sometimes said her mind seemed a million miles away. That was something she couldn't imagine. A million miles.

"Hello, baby girl," Aunt Mae said from the doorway. "Just look at how you've grown." She planted a kiss on Edna's cheek, then poured herself a cup of coffee and sat down.

Mother said something to her and she replied, but Edna paid no attention.

Aunt Mae thought she had grown. Edna straightened and grinned. No one had said anything about her growing, though she prayed nightly to get taller. After all, she would be seven in July. Petite, like her mother, everyone said, but she wanted to be tall like her father. Not even Mother or Daddy had mentioned her growing. But to be fair it had been dark when they climbed down from the train and Daddy had swung her up into his arms.

Then he'd started to cough and Mother had taken her, set her on her feet. "She's too big to carry, Finas."

Well, that much was good, wasn't it? Too big to carry. That must mean she'd grown some. But that had been the only reference to her size. Even though she did want to grow, she never wanted to be too big for Daddy to carry. He coughed a lot and it made her afraid that her parents' secret was much worse than she thought.

Because of his sickness, Daddy had to pay someone a dollar a day and board. She'd heard him talking about how thirty dollars a month cut into his pension. She wasn't sure what a pension was, but gathered it had something to do with his time in the war. As for board, she had no idea at all. What kind of a board would someone want for doing work?

While she thought this over and ate her breakfast, Aunt Mae and Mother chatted. Outside Daddy and Gus—the man who got paid a dollar a day and board—left in the wagon to go to Taos Junction to bring back drinking water.

When the clatter of wheels passed out of hearing, she spooned the last of the oatmeal into her mouth. Time to call up the horses and see if Major had changed.

Outside, someone whooped and hollered. Still chewing the last of her breakfast, Edna scooted from her chair and ran to the door, pursued by Mother and Aunt Mae.

"It's that Marcum woman," Aunt Mae said. "Drunk again. Oh, dear, I hope she doesn't have that awful pistol."

An Indian woman, wearing a white apron over a riding skirt with glasses perched on her nose, rode bareback into the yard. Arms waving like mad, she rode with her legs pinned around the belly of a small pinto horse. In one hand she held the dreaded pistol and fired it into the air.

Aunt Mae hollered and covered her face, only to peer between her fingers as if afraid she'd miss something. Edna's heart thundered in her chest. In Kentucky she'd missed Lily's visits, but dared not say so.

She caught her breath when the woman wheeled the horse in great circles, its hooves sending up chunks of earth. Lily leaned so far to one side, then the other, that her long dark braid swept trails in the dust.

Oh, dear. What if she fell off?

"Get back in here, child," Mother shouted, "before she shoots you."

Mother and Aunt Mae dragged her inside by the arms and slammed the door, then crouched below the window to peer over the sill. Standing back a ways, Edna watched the exciting show. Lily Marcum continued what Mother called her shenanigans for a bit longer, then rode off, her whoops fading into the distance.

Outside was where all the action was, so Edna broke free and ran back onto the porch, but all that was left of Lily was a swirling drift of dust.

Disappointed, she ducked back inside in time to hear the older women lamenting about the Indian girl's behavior.

"Got into the vanilla extract again, I expect," Mother said with a shake of her head.

"Poor John. Next time he'll think twice before he trades a perfectly good wagon for such as that."

"Well, she is young and pretty."

"You can bet she satisfies his needs, even if she does chew tobacco and spit and curse like a man."

Mother frowned, adjusted her glasses and tipped her head toward Edna. But Aunt Mae kept on like she'd been wound up and couldn't stop.

"I'd say it serves him right. Trading a wagon for a wife, and an Indian at that. I wish she wouldn't fire that gun around decent folk. One day she's liable to kill someone with it."

Mother eased toward the window to make sure Lily had gone.

"Fine thing," Aunt Mae remarked, "when our only neighbor within miles is a drunken Indian living in sin with a man nearly twice her age."

That earned her another scowl from Mother. "Mae, shush, please."

"I want to ride like that one day," Edna said, and both women stared hard at her. "Well, I do."

The way they glared at her, eyes big and mouths pursed, she decided not to tell them about Tobe Marcum and the arrowheads he brought her. How he came sneaking up so no one would see. He was a good friend, and she enjoyed his tales, but sensed Mother and Daddy would not approve.

Mother came away from the window and dusted at her dress like it might have been soiled by Lily's presence. "I saved you some scraps of fabric to make fairy clothes. Let's get them out and you can sew while Aunt Mae and I talk."

She knew what that meant. She was no longer welcome in the room with the grown-ups. It didn't matter, though; if she wanted to she could listen in on their talk without them ever knowing it. Sometimes they gossiped about boring stuff and she preferred to make up her own stories. But this business about Lily Marcum was interesting, though she didn't truly understand all of it.

"Swears like a man, too. Bet his wife is turning over in her grave," Aunt Mae whispered.

"I know, I know. Perhaps we could talk about something else."

Aunt Mae shushed and they began to chatter about their failure to figure out how to bake a decent cake in this altitude.

Shrugging, Edna picked up a piece of pale yellow cloth sprinkled with tiny blue flowers. It would be pretty for Kathleen, the smallest member of the fairy family that lived in the woods. And when Mother said her name with what Daddy called her charming Irish brogue, Edna envisioned the little sprite in her mind's eye, wild red hair and green eyes, beautiful crystal clear wings that shimmered in the sunlight, and so tiny she could perch on the end of her little finger.

She rubbed the material. Yes, this would make a fine dress for Kathleen.

It was late when Cassie heard the wagon coming. Gus would unhitch the team and turn them out. She slid Finas' supper from the warming oven, set it on the table and poured him a cup of coffee. She could hear him coughing as he clomped up the steps. The high altitude and fresh air might be good for him, but the hard work wasn't. Still she couldn't get him to "laze around," as he put it. He only hired help because he couldn't physically keep up with all the jobs on this homestead that would be theirs one day, if it didn't kill or bankrupt them first.

"A man stays healthy when he works," he'd said so many times she heard it in her sleep. In her nightmares as well, for often she dreamed of his death and of the suffering he would endure.

Rubbing her forehead, she put on a smile and turned to greet him when he came through the door.

His wide-set, soulful eyes brightened and he held out open arms. Never demonstrative in public, he was very much so in private, and with the baby in bed, he would want to hold her. She welcomed his arms enclosing her, strong despite his illness. The day had been long and lonely, except for the excitement created by Lily Marcum's visit.

After embracing her he washed his hands and face, toweled them dry and sat down at the table. She settled beside him, close enough their knees touched.

"Who did you see today?"

Shoveling a spoonful of stew into his mouth, he chewed and swallowed before replying. "The usual. Wagons lined up with freight, wood, coal and lumber to load on board."

"By the usual you mean all the homesteaders were there for their ration of water and a good long gossip session."

He smiled and she smiled back. One thing for sure. The good Lord knew they understood each other, and that was a blessing, considering the life he'd chosen for them. Why he thought they could make a go of this homestead when there was no water confused her. How she longed for a hot bath in more than a pan of water.

The train hauled drinking and cooking water to Taos Junction from Alamosa once a week and they paid thirty-five cents a barrel for it. By being frugal they could make a barrel last a week. Stock water they hauled from John Marcum's tanks two-and-a-half miles away, and to be sure they kept a barrel under the down spout to catch rainwater. When and if there was any.

They weren't the only ones who'd taken the government up on its offer of free land. Other young World War One vets had signed up for land, but she hadn't met all of them. Finas had told her that they were mostly from Central Texas and were well-educated, from good Protestant backgrounds, for the most part not married. Grubbing sagebrush to clear pastureland from dawn to dusk wasn't what they'd expected, and maybe none of them would stay. Ashamed, she prayed that might happen and she and Finas could follow suit.

She listened to him talk, more for the low-pitched and soothing sound of his voice than for what he had to say. Sometimes she thought he was probably the kindest man she'd ever met. Other times he could be so stubborn she wanted to scream at him to get some sense in that thick head of his.

With the spoon halfway to his mouth, Finas said, "Long John was there."

"Oh?" She waited, knowing what was coming. Finas did not appreciate the man who had nearly single-handedly built this part of the country. "And how is Mr. Dunn?"

"A braggart, as usual. I do wish he wouldn't speak of his wife in such a derogatory way. He might do better if someone would wash his mouth out with soap."

She couldn't help but laugh at such a notion.

He finished chewing. "It's not funny. The man is a bigot as well. It's a wonder to me someone hasn't shot him by now. Going around telling folks he licked three Mexicans before breakfast as if it were something to be proud of."

Though she ought to know better than to play the devil's advocate with her husband, she couldn't help voicing her own opinion. "I expect it takes a man like that to accomplish what he has."

"Oh? A man couldn't build an empire without badmouthing the hardworking poor and mistreating his wife? I think he could."

"All the same, without him there wouldn't be a stage line or a bridge over the Rio Grande River or a mail route in these parts."

"Yes, well...in case you didn't know it, he didn't build that bridge, he rookered a fella named Meyers out of it. All he did was steal it then make honest folks pay to use it." Finas shoveled his stew as if it were rocky soil and chewed with angry deliberation until he'd cleaned the bowl and finished a large slab of bread. "You ask me, he's a criminal, plain and simple."

Though Cassie hadn't been around Long John Dunn much, she admired his accomplishments. To her he looked like Groucho Marx. And he did own the only car in the country, a Pierce Arrow. But she wasn't willing to stand up for him against her own husband. So instead she told him about her day and how Lily Marcum had paid a visit.

The story changed his mood and he chuckled. "She offered Ben and me some of her home brew while you were gone after Edna. I never told you, did I?"

"Finas, you didn't...?"

"Well, not exactly. She makes it out of tank water. Neither of us wanted to die of a drink of bad whiskey."

He kept his eyes on the table, and so she knew there was more to the story.

"She pulled that blamed pistol on us and forced us to take a drink."

"Finas Smith. That sounds like a bad joke. I'm not sure I believe you. However, I see it didn't kill you, but it would've served you right if it had."

He laughed so hard tears ran from his eyes, but he didn't say different.

Cassie gathered the dishes and fiddled with a spoon. "That boy of John Marcum's, he comes over once in a while and brings Edna arrowheads. She doesn't think I know, but I've kept an eye on his comings and goings. Even though she needs friends, I don't like him being around her. He's at least twelve."

He sobered. "I don't like it either, but I do hate to chase away a friend of hers. You continue to keep a close eye on him."

"Oh, believe me, I will."

"Has he ever done anything out of the way?"

"No, and he won't either."

He finished his coffee and handed her the cup. "John must enjoy Lily's company. None of our business, I don't suppose."

"All the same, I wish she'd stay home, and that boy too." She rose, set the dirty dishes in the dishpan and poured hot water over them.

He came up behind her and untied her apron. "Won't those wait till morning?"

Heat crawled up her neck and she turned into his embrace.

"Indeed they will," she whispered against the sun-bronzed skin at his throat.

Edna had never had a pet. She didn't even own a horse of her own, though she yearned for one. Daddy said she was too young and she could ride on Major with him, anyway. She settled for riding a stick horse and pretending. Her imagination, fueled by her Mother's own make-believe games, made of the stick a great black stallion who could race with the wind across the desert.

One morning she followed Mother to the chicken pen and was helping scatter feed around when she spied a little yellow chick turning in circles while the others ran hither and yon around an old mother hen. To her dismay, one of the hens pecked at the baby, driving it hard into the ground.

"Shoo, you nasty old thing." She waved her arms to chase the hen away, then bent down and touched the top of the fuzzy yellow head.

He peeped loudly and kept turning circles. Something was wrong with him. It was a rule that they didn't make pets out of the animals. Still, surely this would be different. She curled her fingers around the warm, soft little body and held it close to her cheek.

"Edna, what're you doing?"

"Something's wrong with him."

Mother took the chick and looked him over closely. "Ah, see here. He has a withered leg. He'll never live to grow up."

She put him down and continued feeding the chickens gathered around pecking at the grains of corn, like she didn't even care.

Here came that nasty old red hen again, wings spread, cawing loudly as she made for the baby. Again Edna snatched it up and kicked at the flogging bird. "Why is she doing that?"

"Because animals don't tolerate the weak or injured or sick."

"Mother." Edna cuddled the baby chick and glared first at the old hen who watched her with beady eyes, then at her mother, who finished scattering grain like nothing was wrong. Tears ran down her cheeks. "Well, I'm sure glad sick people aren't flogged and killed." With that pronouncement, she turned and ran to the house sobbing.

Mother said no more about her keeping the crippled chick.

However, she didn't allow Peeper to stay in the house, so Edna made a small pen in one corner of the barn where he'd be safe from the other chickens. It wasn't long before he lost all his baby fuzz and sprouted beautiful bronze feathers. Every morning she went out to hold and talk to him.

One morning after her chores, she ran into the cool darkness to play with Peeper. But he was gone. She searched everywhere in the barn where the smell of hay and horses and leather hung thick like dust. Major looked up and whinnied at her.

"What are you doing in here? You ought to be out in the pasture." She swung open the stall and there on the floor between his hooves lay Peeper...or what was left of him. Major had stepped on him.

Dropping to her knees she touched the still form. Poor little

Peeper was cold and still. Scooping him up, she cuddled him. His head hung limply from her hand.

"Peeper. Peeper." She shook him. Surely he would awaken, though she'd never seen him lie so still, not even making a sound or opening an eye to peer at her.

Major lowered his velvety nose to sniff at Peeper, then snorted and backed off.

"Shame on you, Major. Get away. Go on."

Tossing his head, Major danced away from her and she rubbed a finger over Peeper's chest.

She knew about dead, but didn't understand it. In school they had learned that some of the people they read about in history books were dead. That meant they were gone away and wouldn't come back. But Peeper was still there, lying in her hand. She didn't know what to do, but deep down inside something crumbled and she started to cry.

"Baby, what's wrong?" Daddy had come into the barn without her hearing him.

Rising from her knees she ran to him, held out the bird. "Make him wake up, Daddy. Make him wake up. Major stomped him."

He knelt, curled one arm around her shoulders and inspected the chick. "Oh, baby, I can't. Your Peeper's gone now. He's dead."

She began to cry so hard she could scarcely breathe. Daddy held her close, patted her back and told her about dying.

"You mustn't blame Major. He probably didn't even see your little chick. I know you're sad, but everyone and everything dies, darling. With people it means our souls have passed on to a better place. But with animals, like your Peeper, here, well, animals live and die in a short time. It doesn't do to get too attached."

"Not even to Major?"

He patted her head. "Not even to Major. Now, dry your eyes and let's put the little bird out back, and think no more about him."

Daddy did not abide much sass, so she let him have Peeper, and tried not to think about him lying dead in the dirt. Like Daddy said, it wasn't easy, something she loved dying.

Chapter Four

Living out here is even more difficult than I supposed. I wouldn't mind so much for myself as for Edna. She gets so lonely. Times are hard. Even with Finas' Army service pension of $45 and health care pension of another $20 every month, sometimes we barely get along. Odd that we're looked on as well-off by some. Because of the TB, we always have to pay someone to help Finas on the ranch. Yet I am determined to make the best of this situation. It is what Finas wants and needs, and I mustn't be selfish. There are many good days.

Often Finas and Cassie sat on the porch after they put Edna to bed. It gave them an opportunity to discuss their day out of their daughter's hearing.

"Such an inquisitive child," Cassie said.

"That means she'll learn more."

"I hope that's all it means. You know my stories of the fairies in the woods? Sometimes I'm afraid I might go too far to entertain her. Perhaps she needs to know more of the real world."

"Time enough for that. She's only a baby. What about the fairies?"

Cassie stared up into the sky, so crowded with stars only patches of darkness filtered through. "Well, she came back from leaving the clothes she'd made—I always pick them up later—and she said she'd looked all around and couldn't find any fairy tracks."

He chuckled, touched her knee and left his broad hand there.

Warmth spread over Cassie. "She'd been listening to you and the other men talk about tracking animals and asked me why fairies didn't leave tracks."

"That's wonderful. So what did you say'?"

"I told her something must have rubbed them out in the night. But the next time I'll make sure and make some tiny tracks."

His hand moved slowly up her thigh. "Why, Cassie. I thought a sweet Irish lass like you believed in the little people. And I guess I always figured fairies had wings."

Odd she hadn't come up with that explanation. Perhaps he had more imagination than she thought. "You're worse than any Irishman filled with blarney, Finas Smith. Now stop rubbing on my leg and let's go to bed."

"Exactly what I had in mind." He grinned and stood, reaching down for her.

"Who is this woman, anyway?" Cassie asked when Finas returned from hauling water to announce they were invited to a party. "No one around here has parties."

"Well, Mrs. Keys does. Something about having bought a piano and she wants to celebrate its arrival. Says it'll be the only piano within fifty miles."

"How in the world did she get it here in one piece?"

He shrugged. "Like everything else. Train and wagon. Anyway, it's Saturday evening. I told her I didn't know if we could come."

Cassie bit her tongue to keep from yelling at him. "Of course, we can go. But who is she?"

"A homesteader."

"You mean her husband is a homesteader."

"No, I mean she is. And I hear her daughter filed on an adjoining 640 acres as well. They're schoolteachers." He notched an eyebrow. "You really want to go?"

"Finas Smith. I haven't seen another woman but Mae in months unless you count that poor Lily Marcum, and you ask me that?" It was her turn to raise her brows. "We can go, can't we?"

"I suppose, if you want."

Though Cassie liked to look presentable, she never fussed much about dressing fancy or wearing gee-gaws. Let her mother and sisters put on airs. To attend the party, she freshened the dress she wore to Sunday services, a simple navy blue linen piped in white, slipped into a pair of rayon stockings and her best shoes, ran a comb through her curly hair and was ready to go.

Finas changed from his usual ranch attire, jeans and a white shirt, to a pair of peg-leg pants and a white shirt. Instead of his usual cowboy hat, he wore a cocky, snap-brim cap. He fitted it just so on his head as they walked to the wagon.

They rode over to the Key's place with M.B. and Mae. She had really gussied up for the occasion, decked out in a long-waisted cream silk dress, a strand of pearls knotted in the low-cut vee at her bustline, and a matching cloche hat. Her bone shoes sported two-inch heels.

Mrs. Keys greeted them at the door. She was a tall, awkward woman, not at all handsome, but pure honey poured forth when she spoke. She was truly a belle of the old South, who might be imagined serving tea on the verandah of her plantation. She wore a long flowing white dress.

"I'm so pleased you could come," she drawled. "Do come in. Would you like some refreshment?"

Cassie followed her trailed by Mae and the reluctant M.B. and Finas. Both men looked as if they'd rather be dragging sagebrush.

If some of the other homestead boys felt that way when they entered the parlor of Kate Keys, they soon changed their minds. Cassie watched with amusement as one after the other preened before Sarah, Kate's twenty-one-year-old daughter, a comely girl who must have inherited her absent and unknown father's good looks. She had high cheekbones and finely drawn features, framed by silken dark hair, waved and spit curled. Unlike her mother, she dressed in the latest flapper fashion, exposing her knees.

Finas and M.B. brought Cassie and Mae some refreshment from a large punch bowl, then, duty done, retired to a corner with some other ranchers to discuss the weather and cattle prices.

The party was a gala affair, but Cassie couldn't take her eyes off the piano. What a grand and beautiful instrument it was. Sarah entertained everyone by playing quite deftly. Cassie recognized the lovely strands of Chopin, having learned the classics growing up in Casselton.

Watching the precocious young Sarah trail her long, delicate fingers over the keys, Cassie wished she had paid more attention to her own music lessons while growing up. How she yearned for such a piano in her own home.

Sipping at a ruby red concoction in the long-stemmed crystal glass, she closed her eyes and was carried far away from this barren place. The magic of Chopin's exquisite polonaise coaxed her into another world.

"Do you like it?" a voice drawled.

She opened her eyes to peer up at Kate Keys. "Oh, yes, it's lovely."

"The only one in this part of the state, I'd wager. And doesn't Sarah play well?"

"Oh, she certainly does," Cassie murmured, then spoke her thoughts aloud. "Perhaps there are other such pianos, with all the artists living in Taos."

"Do you know of another?" Clearly, the woman was displeased to have her opinion challenged.

"I...no, of course not. The music carried me away and I forgot my manners. It was so nice of you to invite us. I understand you and your daughter teach school."

"Oh, yes, we do. In Tennessee. That's why we're often gone." She paused, eyes glittering. "I invited everyone, you know."

Cassie smiled tightly. The woman had certainly put her in her place, as much as saying the Smiths were nobody special. She shouldn't have made the remark about the piano. Never mind, it didn't matter. Mrs. Keys' manners were lacking as well, for she hadn't even asked Cassie her name.

"Yes, that was very nice of you. You have a lovely home."

"Where do you live?" Kate asked, her eyes busily surveying the room, chin held high.

"A few miles north of Taos Junction. We're homesteading."

"Isn't everyone? All those tacky little tar-paper shacks," Kate drawled, then moved away, calling someone's name.

"Nice to have met you, too," Cassie muttered, and drank the remainder of her punch in quick gulps.

Soon she and Mae sat in a remote corner with Mrs. Patchen and Mrs. Wilton, the women who lived in Taos Junction.

"Doesn't it ever rain here?" Cassie asked.

"This has been a very dry year," Mrs. Wilton said. "Normally we have more snow and rain than we've had these past years."

"I've tried to raise a little garden," Cassie said, "but there's just not enough water left over to keep it alive. It's mostly dying or dead already."

Mrs. Wilton nodded. "Yes, and too bad. I remember when we first came here we grew some wonderful cabbages and potatoes, even pumpkins and squash. But you're right, this year the gardens haven't done well at all."

"I wonder what we'll have for Thanksgiving dinner this year? Surely no one has a turkey?" Mae looked at Cassie and winked.

Cassie shook her head slightly and frowned. If Mae volunteered them for turkey duty again, she'd strangle her.

"I expect we could find one somewhere. You girls did such a good job last year, I wouldn't be surprised if you weren't asked to volunteer again." Mrs. Patchen couldn't hide her own amusement.

"I really think a roast of lamb would be delicious," Cassie said.

Mae laughed and the other ladies joined her.

That fall, Edna was enrolled in the little one-room school at Taos Junction. She was in the second grade. Once her name was safely written down in the teacher's book, she breathed a great sigh of relief. She had been so afraid Mother and Daddy would send her back to Kentucky to school. Living here was so much more fun.

One day she went in Mr. Henery's store with Daddy. It smelled of feed and tobacco and some mysterious scents she couldn't put a name to. She wandered slowly through, admiring straw hats and bandanas, open barrels of pickles and bins of crackers. The old floorboards squeaked underfoot.

She rounded a corner and saw a beautiful young Indian girl with long, shiny black hair standing near a large bin of sugar. She glanced around with wide, brown eyes, as if afraid someone might be watching her. The pretty girl wore a blue and red dress and knee-high leather moccasins with intricate beadwork.

Edna drew up short and peered from behind a shelf containing a neat stack of overalls. Just as she was about to step out into the aisle to admire the boots, the girl dipped out a scoop of sugar and poured it into the top of one of her mocassin boots. Darting a quick glance in all directions, she dug out another scoop and did the same thing.

Should she go tell Daddy? Edna wondered. How funny that sugar must feel squishing around her feet. Why did she have to do that? Perhaps she couldn't pay, or maybe she wanted to see if she could get away with stealing. Eating sugar that had been in her shoes held no appeal at all for Edna.

Before she could decide what to do, the girl ran through the store and out the door. She never told Mother or Daddy about what she'd seen, but often thought of how bad it would be to have to steal sugar and carry it around in her shoes.

Soon she got acquainted with the children who lived in the area. There weren't many, but there was a Miller child in every grade from first to eighth. Jane was in second grade with her and they played together at recess every day. She told Edna there were ten Miller children, eight of them in school. One too young and another too old.

About the third week after school started, the teacher announced that she had been instructed on how to give immunization shots to all the students. Each child was given a slip of paper to take home asking for their parents' consent.

The next day everyone returned their signed consent slips except the Miller children.

When asked why, Jane stood up, hands locked behind her back and said, "My daddy said that by God, none of us was going to be stuck with a needle. No sir." Her dark hair fell over her face as she sat back down and stared at her lap.

Nothing more was said, and when the other children lined up to be "stuck" the Miller children remained in their seats.

A few weeks later, Miss Hankins stood in front of the class once again, thin features drawn.

"I don't want any of you to worry, but there's been an outbreak of typhoid fever. Immunizations will be given here at the school tomorrow evening. It's important that everyone get their shot." She passed among the students, handing each of them an announcement to take home. "Make sure your parents come as well."

She paused beside Jane's desk. "Please tell your father how important this is, Jane." Placing the slip on the girl's desk, she moved on.

On the playground after lunch, Edna approached Jane. Though she had no idea what typhoid fever was, it worried her that her best friend might take it and die. They sat together for a while in silence, then Edna said, "Is your dad going to let you get the shot?"

"I don't think so."

"None of you?"

"Nope." Jane scooped a handful of sand into a pile, not looking at Edna.

"But what if you all die?"

Jane shrugged. "I don't know. Maybe we will."

"Are you scared?"

"Nope."

Edna nodded somberly, thinking of her pet chicken and how cold and limp the little bird had been after Major stepped on him. She could hardly imagine Jane looking like that. Tears came to her eyes and she wiped them away with her fist.

At home that evening, she told Mother and Daddy about the Millers.

Daddy put an arm around her. "Well, honey, you know we can't make others do something because we think it's right. They have a right to their own decisions."

"But what if they're wrong? And what if they all die?"

"Well, sweetheart, I don't think they'll all die. Besides, they can be wrong if they want to be. We can't do anything about it."

Edna teared up. "I don't want Jane to die, or Emmy Lou or Sarah or the boys, either."

"No one does, honey."

"I don't think their daddy cares or he'd let them have the shots."

Daddy glanced at Mother. "Of course, their daddy cares. He doesn't want them to die."

"What is typhoid, anyway?"

"Your territory, dear," Daddy said.

Mother dried her hands from washing dishes and sat down near Edna and Daddy. "It's a disease carried by bad little bugs. We can't see them, so we have to get immunized against their attack."

"Where do they come from? Do they bite?"

"Sometimes they get in water or milk, and it gets infected…dirty, and we drink it, then we get sick. They don't bite. Others can get sick by being around those who are infected."

Edna squeezed her daddy's knee. "Then, if Jane gets sick I can't be around her?"

Cassie took her by the shoulders. "I don't want you worrying about this anymore. No one is getting sick. We'll all go get our immunizations tomorrow and everything will be fine."

"But Jane's Daddy won't let them."

"That can't be helped. Now why don't you come help me dry the dishes?"

Edna looked at Daddy, wishing he would say something more.

He did, but it didn't help much. "Go on, child. Help your mother, and leave the worrying to us, okay? Maybe someone will talk to Mr. Miller and he'll change his mind."

"Finas," Mother said in her stern voice.

"Help your mother," he said and lifted his Zane Grey novel, a sign she was not to bother him anymore.

"But, I don't want—"

"Edna, that's enough now," Mother said, and handed her the dish towel.

The next evening a crowd of parents and children gathered at the school, lined up and got their shots. Edna watched with dwindling hope, but the Millers never came. The needle hardly hurt at all, and she couldn't understand Mr. Miller's ideas.

A week went by and all the Miller children were at school every day, showing no sign of being sick. Maybe the bugs didn't get close to them.

She and Jane played jump rope at recess every day and she watched her closely. She looked fine. It was going to be okay, for sure. No one would get the typhoid fever. Then, Monday, Jane and her littlest brother William, who was in first grade, were absent. She stared with horror at the empty seats. By Friday, their sister June, who was in the third grade, didn't come to school.

Frightened and filled with sorrow, Edna asked one of the older boys, who was in the eighth grade and sullen, but he only muttered, "They's sick."

She went home and told her parents that three Miller children had typhoid fever.

"My goodness, child. Who told you that?" Mother said.

"Nobody. But they're not in school and Zeke said they're sick."

"Well, maybe…it could be anything."

But it wasn't. A week later, on a Thursday morning, none of the Miller children came to school.

Suppose they all had the typhoid fever? What if they all died? Edna could hardly sit still in her seat.

Miss Hankins again stood in front of the class to make an announcement. Her face looked so bad Edna knew it was something terrible. She wanted to run from the room or cover her ears. It made her stomach hurt. At the same time, she had to know what was wrong. What a terrible way to feel. Wanting not to know and needing to know, all at the same time.

"Class, I'm sorry to have to tell you that one of your classmates has passed on."

Passed on? Did that mean died?

Everyone murmured, looked around at the empty seats.

Edna twisted her hands in her lap. Why didn't Miss Hankins say who it was?

"Little June Miller has died of typhoid fever. Now, I don't want any of you to be frightened. You've all had your immunizations. We see just how important they were, don't we?"

Edna waved her hand in the air, then stood when Miss Hankins nodded and said her name.

"Miss Hankins, what about Jane and William?"

"I'm told they are recovering, and none of the others have taken ill, so it should have passed them by." She gazed across the classroom, then turned and picked up a book. "All right, let's get to work on our geography."

All the Millers returned to school the following week, except for Jane and William, who were still recovering from the fever, and of course June, who was dead. Edna made friends with a couple of other girls near her age, and when Jane did come back, she looked older, sadder. She stayed to herself a lot and never played much the rest of the school year. Edna didn't blame her. It was because her little sister had died and it was her daddy's fault. That would be a hard thing. A really hard thing.

Cassie always welcomed Finas' return from Taos Junction. While he and a couple of hands unloaded the water, she made tea and poured him a cup of coffee from the percolator on the stove top. When he came into the kitchen, she stood at the counter, mixing up a batch of cornbread and pretending disinterest. He knew, though, that she could hardly wait for him to entertain her with stories he'd heard in town.

On this particular early November day, he hugged his cup of hot coffee, features lined with amusement.

"You remember Mrs. Keys and her piano?"

"I remember," she said, tightening her lips.

"Well, it seems when she and Sarah went off to teach school in September, she decided to let the Miller family have the piano for the winter. It wouldn't do it much good sitting in an unheated house."

"The Millers? The bootleggers?"

"The very same."

"Quite a choice."

"Some of the hands thought so too. In fact a few of the boys decided that wasn't the best element in which to keep such a treasured instrument, what with the comings and goings of such a rough element. So they took it upon themselves to go over to the Millers to retrieve the piano."

"Oh, my goodness." Cassie drew up a chair and sat near Finas, sipping from her cup of tea.

"Indeed. Well, it was Norbert who told the story, but he just went along for backup. Cletus took his wagon to haul it away in, and I don't know who else went along. They were laughing so hard in the telling, I didn't catch who got horsewhipped, but—"

"Horsewhipped? But that's awful. That terrible Mr. Miller."

"Don't jump to conclusions, it wasn't Mr. Miller. Just let me tell this. It seems Cletus, the other two men at his back, goes up and knocks and says politely, 'Mrs. Keys asked me to take her piano home as she will be coming in soon for the holidays.'"

"And so, that sounds reasonable." Cassie blew on her tea and waited. Finas had a way of dragging out his tales.

"Yes, it does, doesn't it?" He drank some coffee and began to chuckle. "I'd a liked to have seen what happened next."

"Me too. In fact, I'd like to know what happened next."

"Oh, yes. Well, Minnie...Mrs. Miller, come raring out of that house with a six-foot-long snake whip, run them boys up into the wagon and snapped it over their heads till the frightened horses just ran right off with them."

"She didn't? Oh, my word." Cassie joined Finas laughing. "Well, so they didn't get the piano?"

"No. Minnie said she'd give it to no one but Mrs. Keys. So I reckon she will have to go fetch it herself when she gets home. Them old boys said they wasn't in any mood to argue with Minnie Miller and her snake whip."

That Sunday the southern gospel singers came to church. Following services and a pot luck dinner, everyone gathered round the pump organ to listen to them sing and even joined in when they knew the words.

The pump organ was the only musical instrument anywhere around except for Mrs. Keys' piano. Mother said that was because organs weren't expensive.

"I'd wager organ salesmen worked overtime going to Sunday sings to make sure everyone bought one," she told Edna. "There's probably a pump organ in every church in New Mexico and Texas."

Daddy laughed, but Edna didn't know what was funny.

She was accustomed to eavesdropping on her parents' private conversations. The house was too small to avoid hearing things she probably wasn't supposed to hear. Like the time they were arguing over all the magazines Daddy received in the mail every month.

"They're expensive, Finas. A newspaper and all these magazines every month. Sometimes it's hard to stretch the food, let alone buying these."

"Nonsense. We're not going hungry. I could be like some of the other men." Even when arguing, Daddy spoke in a soft tone, but sometimes, like now, he clipped his words.

"What has that got to do with anything?" Mother often spoke more harshly than him.

"Well, most of the men we know buy beer and sometimes even go to Lily for moonshine. I think reading material is a lot more important than a swig of beer, don't you?" Daddy started coughing and Mother waited until he stopped before replying.

"Certainly. Of course, I do, if we could afford the beer and spent it instead on magazines. But we can't afford either. Things are getting tough."

Edna scooted closer to the open door. What things were tough? She didn't know what Mother was talking about.

"I know, sweetheart. But we have so much more than most do out here. Why, I'm considered rich compared to some. There's my pension and then the disability from the army. Not many have monthly cash coming in despite whatever else happens." He succumbed to another fit of coughing.

"This place is killing you."

"Has nothing to do with the magazines, though, does it?"

Edna could barely hear her mother's reply. "No, I don't guess it does."

Chapter Five

Cassie's Journal—1922

How sad that we are always leaving Edna or taking her away somewhere. I often wonder what it will do to her to live with so many different people. Maybe one day she will no longer love me or look at me as her mother. I truly pray that never happens, for it seems our life is doomed to be one of constant change.

"We're only going to leave you in Servilleta for a little while." Without looking at Edna, Mother folded her clothes and packed them into a small satchel. "You must be brave. Your father has been called in to work for a couple of months and I'm going to Santa Fe to nurse at the hospital there. Then we'll come and get you and we'll go back to the ranch."

"What about the house and the animals, the horses...Major?" Tear welled in her eyes and her heart ached.

"Edna, please," Mother said. "It's only for a little while. Gus will see to feeding the stock."

Seated in the wagon she watched the house and barn fade behind them, and fought sobs that jerked at her chest. This wasn't fair. Why did Mother and Daddy have to go away to work?

They were going to leave her again, this time in Servilleta where she would stay with Mrs. Perkins in her boarding house. Only for a little while. She didn't want to be a baby, she really didn't, but why couldn't she go with them? She would soon be eight years old. Why did little kids always have to be left out of grown-up affairs? Maybe if she was big enough, brave enough, they would come for her soon.

But what if they never came back? Each time they left, she was afraid they wouldn't come home. What would she do?

Daddy took a deep breath and lay his hand over hers. "It'll be all right, baby. It's only for a little while. You be a big girl, now."

If she was truly a big girl, then they'd take her with them, wouldn't they?

Mother stared straight ahead and said no more.

At the train station she waved goodbye to her parents until the train went out of sight, then buried her face in Mrs. Perkins' apron and cried. Lena Jo, Mrs. Perkins' daughter, who was older than her and much more grown up, patted her back.

"It'll be okay, you'll see."

Edna straightened. Be big, be brave. She'd almost forgotten.

"Well, come on then," Mrs. Perkins said. "Let's get back to the house. There's work to do." She hustled the girls away.

Edna couldn't stop looking over her shoulder at the train growing smaller and smaller, like her heart.

Lena Jo took her hand and pointed at a long row of pens. "That's where John Sargent puts his sheep. We'll come to town to watch them drive the herd in. So many sheep you can't even count them. And do they ever make a racket."

"Why does he bring them here?" Edna sniffled.

"He ships them off on the train."

"Why?" Despite her sorrow, Lena Jo had perked her interest.

The girl shrugged. "I really don't know. I expect people in other places want them for something. When he brings them to town we have to move out of our house for about three weeks. It belongs to Mr. Sargent and he needs it while he and his men are here."

"My goodness, where do you live?"

"One of the homesteaders loans us his shack. It's kind of like camping out. And it's not for long. It'll be fun, you'll see."

"Where does he go?"

"Who?"

"The homesteader."

"Oh, he just moves in with a neighbor. They mostly don't have families, you know. They are young men who have been to war. And

Mama says that now the government is repaying them for risking their lives by giving them this worthless land no one else wants cause there's no water."

Stunned, Edna gazed out across the sagebrush flats she loved so much. Worthless? How could that be?

Without giving Edna a chance to defend her beloved home, Lena Jo pointed at a small building. "And that is Mr. McCracken's store. His son James is my special friend. You'll meet him. There's the school house where John McCracken teaches. He's one of James' older brothers." She shook her head in mock seriousness. "They have nine children, and Mama doesn't know for the life of her where they put them."

Edna didn't either. Nine children all in one house must be crowded. Sometimes she and Mother and Daddy got in each other's way in their small house.

"Back there is the railroad section house. Some kids live there too, with their folks, but not that many. Their dads work for the railroad. Mama runs the boarding house where you'll be staying. There are lots of rooms, but we'll have to share one because lots of travelers stay there too. Some get off the train, others from the road. It's very busy." Lena Jo nodded seriously. "There's plenty for us to do. She'll want you to help me do dishes and make beds, I expect."

Trudging along beside the older girl, Edna listened with half an ear to the chatter. Though some things caught her attention, she didn't care about any of it. Not really. All she wanted was to go with Mother and Daddy. They were going so far away. And she'd never get to visit them, or they her.

"See this road?" Lena Jo's question interrupted her thoughts. "It runs all the way to Santa Fe, just like the train. Plenty of people travel on it and ride the train as well. When they stay overnight with us some of them tell wonderful adventure stories. When we play, James and I and the other kids pretend we are them. You'll like it, I promise you will." Lena Jo squeezed her hand. "Do you like to read? I have so many books and it's fun to read the stories, then act them out."

"My Daddy likes to read too, but I only went through the second grade in Taos Junction, and Mother said I didn't learn much there.

She must be right cause I don't remember learning anything special I didn't already know. I sure wish I could've gone with my daddy."

"Where did he go?"

"To work for the railroad. But I'll only be here a very short time. That's what my mother promised."

"Why did your mother go to?"

"Oh, she's a nurse and she will work at the hospital in Santa Fe."

Lena Jo nodded and began to skip, pulling her along so that soon she was matching the older girl's steps. A gentle wind dried her tears but did nothing for her sorrow.

This place called Servilleta was certainly going to be different from living on the homestead. But it wouldn't be for long, not for long at all. Mother promised.

Lena Jo had been right about everything. Each day she rose early, helped out with the chores, making beds and washing dishes, not her favorite thing, then off they would go—she, Lena Jo, James and the little tag-alongs. As Kings and Queens, sailors, explorers and cowboys and Indians they roamed the countryside on horseback or afoot. While she never stopped longing for home and her mother and daddy, Edna enjoyed those long summer days.

In the evenings after supper, usually shared by up to a dozen people who seemed glad to pay twenty-five cents for the tasty food, she would sit quietly near her new friend and listen to breathtaking tales. Travelers along the mud and stone road that ran from Alamosa past the boarding house and on to Santa Fe appeared to have many adventures. These wondrous tales fueled the children's imagination. Some of them were poor, others rich, most working men, but they all knew about a world that the children had no notion of. While listening to their stories beautiful pictures of far-off places flashed through her head, almost as good as the pictures in Daddy's books and magazines.

It was there, not long after settling in, that she met Sylvester Phillip Astoria, a man she would never forget. And they met in a most unexpected way.

She, Jim, Lena Jo and the tag-alongs galloped their cowboy and Indian game through the front yard of the boarding house, up the steps, all over the porch, then banged through the front door. Such whooping and hollering had never been heard as cowboys shot Indians, horses stampeded and what Indians were left alive, scalped the cowboys in one room after another.

In the parlor sat a tall, mustached gentleman who rose to his feet in indignation when they exploded into his territory.

"What sort of nonsense is this?"

At the deep roar of his voice, all came to an immediate halt. Edna, being the closest to the large gentleman, trembled as she looked up into his scowling face.

Mrs. Perkins scurried in. "Outside, the lot of you. Now."

It seemed a good idea, and they galloped back out onto the porch where they hunkered beside the window to listen.

"I'm so sorry, Mr. Astoria. They're just children."

"Disgusting little urchins, I'd say," he muttered. "Where did they learn their manners?"

None of them could help giggling. Edna had no idea what an urchin was, and neither did any of the others. It wasn't long before they gathered with plans to put on a real show for Mr. Sylvester Phillip Astoria. And so they lay in wait for another opportunity to disgust him further.

"Yeah, just who does he think he is, anyway?" Jim asked.

"Mama says he's a retired officer of His Majesty's Royal Navy," Lena Jo told them.

Edna stopped her right there. "Who is his majesty?"

"Why the King of England, of course."

"I never heard of such a thing." Edna was sure that if Daddy hadn't mentioned a thing, then it didn't exist, and he'd never said anything about a King of England.

"I know it's true," Lena Jo said, swelling up. "He speaks four languages."

"If he's so important what's he doing here?" Jim asked.

Lena Jo shrugged. "Mama says nobody knows how he came to be here, but he has a homestead in the sage brush on the banks of the Rio Grande."

"Is he staying?"

"Mama said he will be here off and on because he travels a lot."

"Next time he comes, let's act really terrible," Jim said.

Lena Jo giggled and punched Jim's arm. "He said we have no manners, well, then, we don't."

Jim laughed and Lena Jo giggled.

"Your mom will get mad at us," Edna said, thinking this was not a good idea at all, yet intrigued by being included in their plans. They were, after all, her best friends.

"Probably," Lena Jo said with a shrug. "But think what fun it will be."

And so the next time Sylvester Phillip Astoria came to stay on his way to Santa Fe, they hatched their plan.

While Edna and Lena Jo crouched outside the open parlor door, Jim raced through, shirttail flying and feet bare. The retired officer of His Majesty's army sat next to another man, expounding about his war experiences.

Jim raised a hand, shouted howdy, ran past the men, then yelled at the girls. "Well, come on, you can't catch me." He then stuck out his tongue and made a rude noise.

Astoria rose to his full height. "See here, young man."

About that time Lena Jo and Edna ran through trailed by the tag-alongs, squealing as loudly as they could.

Whatever Astoria said then couldn't be heard for the noise as they ran two circles yelling, then left the room, pounded down the porch steps and hid behind the house. There they fell to the ground laughing so hard it was almost impossible to take a breath.

Later, Jim had gone home and so missed out on the consequences of their trick, but Edna and Lena Jo faced an angry Mrs. Perkins. She sat them down after supper, when all the boarders had gone to their rooms.

"I have nothing against children having fun, but the two of you carried it way too far today. You insulted one of our guests, and he's a fine gentleman, too."

"We were only playing," Lena Jo said.

Edna decided to keep quiet.

"I think it was more than that, but suppose you were only playing, you know that sort of mischief is not allowed around our boarders. You've been raised better than that, Lena Jo." She then turned to Edna. "And I'm not leaving you out of this, young lady. Your parents would be most distressed to know how you acted today. That was not at all proper."

Lena Jo clearly decided her mother meant business. "Yes, Mom. It wasn't her fault. It was my idea."

"Why, for goodness sake?"

"Mama, he called us urchins, so we thought…"

"So you thought you'd prove him right?"

"No…I mean, yes. I guess."

"Well, you are going to apologize to Mr. Astoria first thing in the morning. No daughter of mine will act like that. You understand me?"

"Yes, Mama."

"Good. Now the two of you, off to bed, and next time keep your shenanigans outside where they belong."

Edna murmured, "Yes, Ma'am," and followed her best friend up the stairs to their room.

After the apology, Mr. Astoria warmed to both girls and entertained them with wonderful stories about far-off places they'd only thought of as storybook fairy tales. He quickly became one of their favorite visitors.

During her time there, Edna met all kinds of people, the great, the small, the bootleggers and governors. In spite of her unhappiness at being away from her parents, it was a great experience.

In September she started to school with nine other children in the small log school house where James' older brother John taught six grades. All the children had so much fun learning and playing that she couldn't think of the days as work. There she truly began to learn and developed a passion for reading that surpassed even that of her best and dearest friend, Lena Jo.

Though the girl was two years older than her, they had grown inseparable. She would have put her head in a lion's mouth if Lena

Jo had asked, and her friend would do the same. She almost forgot that her parents should have returned for her.

The school house was small, and when filled with ten children and a teacher, it was probably a lot like how the McCrackens and their ten children lived every day, crammed all up together, stumbling over each other at every turn. The room contained a raised stage in one end where the teacher could stand, and an organ. For a while she puzzled over what the organ was doing in a school house. That salesman Mother spoke of had certainly gotten around.

Not long after she and the Perkins returned to the eight-room boarding house after Mr. Sargent shipped off his sheep, she found out more about the organ's use. It was then, at the beginning of October that everyone began to talk about Fifth Sunday.

In spite of all the fun, Edna had begun to worry about when Mother and Daddy would be home, and so she listened without much interest. Then Lena Jo's Mama came home one day with a large, brown-paper-wrapped package and summoned the two girls into the dining room. When Edna saw a familiar handwriting, she stretched to see the return address.

Mother! The package was from Mother. She wrote occasionally and the letters would come on the train, but this. A package. She'd never had a package before. What could it be?

Mrs. Perkins lay it on the table and produced a pair of scissors to cut the string. Then she slowly undid both ends. The paper crackled.

Edna could hardly contain herself. Her tongue went dry and her heart beat really fast so she feared losing her breath. When finally Mrs. Perkins revealed the contents, a bundle of splendid blue material, she gasped in wonder.

"Here's her note," Mrs. Perkins said, but when Edna reached for it, she pulled it away, opened it and read:

> *Dear Mrs. Perkins,*
> *I am sending this blue serge for you to make the girls new dresses for Fifth Sunday. I trust our daughter is well and not giving you any trouble. She*

has always been a big help around the house. Tell
her hello and that I want her to be a good girl. I will
write soon and explain our delay in returning.
    I remain, yours truly,
    Cassie Smith

Edna rubbed a hand over the fabric, while Lena Jo danced around jabbering about what kind of dresses they should have. Edna felt the texture of what Mother had called serge, and great tears welled in her eyes. Soon she was sobbing, one hand pressed tight on the bundle.

Mrs. Perkins and Lena Jo gazed at her, both asking what was wrong in unison.

"I wanted her to tell me why they haven't come home. I'm afraid they won't ever come."

"Of course, they will. She'll write soon and explain everything." Mrs. Perkins looked as if she knew much more than she was saying, the way she clamped her lips tight to keep the words from falling out of her mouth.

The letter came in a few days, and it was much worse than she had imagined. Daddy had taken sick and Mother had gone with him down to Ft. Bayard in Silver City so he could go in the hospital and get well. Now they were even farther away.

Edna thought she would never be able to stop crying. Her head and stomach hurt from it. "What if he dies?" she asked between hiccoughing and sobbing.

"Oh, child, no. If he were that sick she would say so. I'm sure he will get better really fast. You mustn't take on so."

Lena Jo patted her arm and hugged her. "Your daddy is going to be just fine. Come on, let's find some pictures of dresses to show Mama how we want ours made."

It wasn't long before Edna was totally entranced by Lena Jo's actions. The girl took the brown paper wrapping and sat down with a pencil. Soon she had drawn them dresses from a picture in a book.

They would be cut like paper doll dresses, straight with a slightly flared skirt and the sleeves also flared. Red yarn would trim the neck tied with pom-pom strings and belts.

"Oh, you wait and see," Lena Jo said, eyes sparkling. "They will be the prettiest dresses ever. Now, come on, let's give this to Mama."

By the time the end of the week before Fifth Sunday rolled around excitement was at such a fevered pitch Edna could barely sit still a minute. She thought about Daddy a lot, but the excitement was just too much to ignore. Such a celebration was something she'd never seen, and no matter how much Lena Jo talked about it, she couldn't envision so may people gathering to sing all day long and eat till they were fit to bust.

The dresses were fitted and finished and hanging in the wardrobe. She didn't think she'd ever seen anything so beautiful. That night the mirror told her a dreadful truth. Her hair was straight and ugly. Mrs. Perkins had kept it cut to the bobbed style she'd worn ever since she could remember her own hair. Oh, how she wished she had Mother's curls.

All it took to get this accomplished was to voice her desire to Lena Jo.

"We'll put our hair up in rags. I know, let's do it tonight. We can leave it up all day Saturday and again all night. Our curls should be so tight they'll dance like springs." She rose and pirouetted around the room in her nightgown, arms flung out like a dancer. "We will be the prettiest girls there."

Lena Jo showed her how to curl separate locks of her dampened hair around a strip of cloth, then tie it down tight until her head was covered with coils tied in colorful rags. Once they both had their hair done up all over, she took a good look at the two of them in the mirror and broke into giggles.

"We look like ragamuffins, I think," she finally managed, not sure exactly what that was, but convinced it fit.

Lena Jo stared at their reflection. "Well, perhaps you're right," she said, putting on her "older than you" act with Edna. "But when we take out the rags I think we'll probably look just like those women who act in moving pictures."

"Oh, do you think so?" Edna tilted her head one way, then another and watched her reflection do the same. She'd never seen a moving picture, couldn't even imagine it, but it must be something grand.

They had both listened enraptured to one of the traveling salesmen who sold ready-to-wear when he bragged about how such women often bought clothes straight from him. He knew a lot about the beautiful women who acted in moving pictures, and the girls would beg him to tell more stories about women with such intriguing names as Gilda Gray and Mae West.

For weeks after his visit, Lena Jo and Edna had paraded around the house "putting-on," as Mrs. Perkins called it.

Studying her small self next to Lena Jo in the mirror, Edna stretched to her tippy-toes, then sighed. "Will I ever grow as tall as you?"

Lena Jo wrapped an arm around her. "I like you just the way you are. You are so delicate and beautiful."

Both girls collapsed in giggles again. They had read the phrase in a book, and true to her personality, Lena Jo hadn't been able to wait until she could use it in a sentence.

Edna threw her arms around her best friend. "I love you, Lena Jo. I always will."

"I love you, too. Now, let's get to bed. I am dreadfully tired."

Edna touched her forehead with the back of her hand. "Yes, I am too. And we must be rested for our appearance Sunday."

Even after the giggles subsided and Lena Jo slept, Edna couldn't relax. Imagining all those people eating dinner on the ground and singing all day, accompanied by the grandest organ music trailed into her dreams.

Cassie gazed at Finas while he slept, traced the bones of his gaunt cheeks. Under her touch his pale skin felt flushed. He dragged in a harsh breath and opened his eyes.

"Hello," she whispered. "How are you today?"

"Fine, I'm fine."

She allowed a glimmer of a smile. He'd be fine the day hell froze over.

"I didn't know if you were coming." He turned away, coughed so hard she hurt for him. She waited patiently, her gaze moving from his sheet-draped form to the white walls of the hospital room.

"What have you been doing?"

She sucked in a breath. "I...I went to the U.S.V.B. hospital today."

His eyes slid sideways to regard her. "And?"

"I...they want me to come to work...tomorrow."

Weak as he was, he closed his hand over hers. "I want you to stay with me and—"

"I know, but they won't let me stay here and take care of you, and other than the short time they will let me in, I'm at loose ends. It's going to be a while before you...before you recover and we can go home."

He rolled his head so he was staring at the opposite wall.

She squeezed his hand, leaned close and smelled the familiar odor of illness and fever.

"I love you, Finas. You need to concentrate on getting well. I'll come as often as they'll let me, I promise. And as soon as you're better, we can go home." She would rather nurse than live on the ranch, and that made her feel ashamed. She must face the reality that he might not make it this time. Instead of showing improvement since she brought him to the hospital, his condition continued to grow worse. She had to be able to take care of herself...and of Edna.

At last he turned back, his eyes glistening with unshed tears. "I'm so sorry about...about all this. I never wanted it to happen. It's not fair to you or to Edna. How is she, by the way?"

"She's fine, and don't change the subject. What's fair got to do with anything?"

"Nothing, I don't suppose. What would you be doing there?"

Relieved, she let out her breath and sat beside him to outline her job at the hospital. "Not exactly the same as in Santa Fe, but it's a good job. I think I'll—"

He drifted off before she finished, and she stood beside him a long while holding his unresponsive hand.

What would she do if he died? Love for him nearly choked her and tears ran down her cheeks.

"Oh, please, my darling. Don't die. Please. I promise I'll live with you anywhere on this earth, if only you'll live. Anywhere, and I'll never complain again."

She leaned down and kissed his fevered cheek, then stumbled from the room. Outside his door, she leaned against the wall and sobbed.

A few days later Cassie spied Finas' doctor as she passed the nurses' station on her way to his room. She so seldom had the opportunity to discuss her husband's condition with him that she made a beeline for the man before he could escape. Perhaps he secretly hid out to keep from talking to someone who knew something about medicine.

He began to speak before she could open her mouth. "His condition has not changed, Mrs. Smith. I'm sorry I can't tell you more."

"So am I. Are you trying new treatments?"

He refused to meet her gaze, shook his head. "I'm afraid we've exhausted everything we can do except keep him comfortable. I think you should face reality. This is a dreadful disease, and he may not make it."

"As long as he draws breath, even be it strained, I have hope. And I won't give up. Perhaps we should take him to another facility, one that is more up-to-date." She glared at him until he raised his eyes.

"Of course, that's up to you. But I wouldn't suggest moving him. In fact, I'll have no part in it. We're doing everything for him that can be done. You know there are no proven treatments for tuberculosis."

Her throat burned and tears threatened. She would not cry in front of this man, no matter what. Besides, he was right. She'd already made inquiries about such a move. She could find no medical consultant who would agree to it. So stay here he would. And she wouldn't leave him. Fear crawled through her that at this very moment Finas could be dying, and her out here arguing with this idiot.

Spinning on her heel, she ran down the hall and into her husband's room. For a long while she stood in the gloom and listened to the rasp of his breathing and allowed her own to settle down.

He slept through her visit, as if to verify her fears, but the next day when she hurried in, she found him sitting in a chair beside the window that was thrown open to let in the fresh air so important to his healing.

He greeted her with forced gaiety. "How are you? You look beautiful."

She went to sit beside him, cupped his hand under hers. "I'm so happy to see you looking better."

"It's a beautiful day." He gazed out the window across the desert. "They wheeled me to the sun porch today. Said I'm to take the air every day, even when I don't feel up to it."

"Oh, I'm so glad. You'll feel better soon, I'm sure." She drew a breath. "I want to tell you something."

He nodded, turned from the scenic view to catch her gaze in his. She saw terror there for an instant before he blinked it away.

"I want to bring Edna here. Well, close by. She needs to be able to visit with you."

Before he could guess at the true reason for bringing Edna there, that she was afraid he'd die without getting to see her, and she him, she hurried on.

"You know she isn't learning much in that little log school, and it'll soon be two years. She's almost ten. These years will be crucial if she's to make something of her life. Besides, I'd like her closer to us."

Maybe he bought the hurried explanation, maybe he didn't. She couldn't tell by his expression.

He squeezed her hand. "I'd like to see her. But where will she stay? What will she do?"

"There's a Catholic boarding school in Silver City. That's nearby and we could see her on weekends and she'd learn something that will stand her in good stead."

Finas chuckled, then fought a paroxysm of coughing before he could speak. "Well, wouldn't that please Mother Cooney?"

Cassie smiled. "Yes, I suppose so, but that isn't the reason."

"Oh, honey. You can't tell me she's not heartbroken that her granddaughter isn't being brought up a good Irish Catholic."

"Perhaps, but that's not the reason." Or was it? Cassie wasn't sure. "It's just that it's close and a good school and—"

"As long as they don't turn her into a nun."

"Of course not. The school was begun to accommodate ranchers' children. I think there are twenty or so girls there. The sisters are from Ireland. It'll be good for her. I just know she's running totally wild at the Perkins'. It's time she began to grow up."

"It would be nice to have her closer. Will they let her see me?"

"Yes, with precautions. Then it's settled. I'll take the train up next week and bring her back with me."

"Are you sure the school can take her?"

Cassie flushed, a little embarrassed. "I already asked. I didn't want to go through this with you if they didn't have room for her."

"In other words, she's already enrolled?"

She nodded, then flashed a wide smile at him.

His answering smile, though weak, encouraged her. Perhaps he would improve with his beloved daughter nearby. He'd always worshiped the very ground she walked on.

She was glad he didn't ask about the homestead. She hadn't been able to bring herself to tell him, but most of the boys who'd filed on the government land had given up the battle. Gus had written, told her there was nothing left on the place. The stock had wandered off, the house was a wreck from vandals. Two years of work, all for nothing. At the moment, she wasn't sure she cared.

All she dreaded was telling Finas about the destruction of his dream. But not now, not yet. She'd made a pact and she would keep her part of the bargain.

She didn't plan to write ahead to inform Edna of their decision to send her to the Catholic school. Monday, she would board the train for the long ride to Servilleta. It would be good to see her daughter after so long a time.

Chapter Six

Cassie's Journal—1923

The Irish Cooneys were among the original settlers of Casselton, North Dakota. Mother was very dictatorial as to how we appeared in public. The good Irish were pulling themselves up by the bootstraps, while the bad Irish were singing in the pubs. Had my father not married the rigidly proper Ellen he would probably have been the best terror of the pub quartet. A couple of the sons had the same problems. Their wives insisted on lace curtains. So when I dared to marry a Methodist cowboy, I had problems with the family bosses. It is a good thing we settled far away.

On board the train, Edna waved and wiped her eyes, then waved again, too choked up to shout the words that crowded into her throat and tried to cut off her breath. Beyond the window, her very best friend in all the world vanished into the distance along with all she'd known in Servilleta.

I love you, Lena Jo. I always will.

Then to Mother: *I don't want to go. Please don't make me go. Why are you doing this to me?*

The mysterious idea of life in a Catholic boarding school terrified her. She didn't even know what a Catholic was.

"They believe in God, but they have funny ways of showing it," Lena Jo had told her. "And nuns give up men and having babies to serve Him."

"What does God have to do with a boarding school?" Edna asked.

"Will I have to work for board, like we wash dishes and make beds at your momma's boarding house? And like Gus did on the ranch?"

Lena Jo studied the problem a moment, then nodded seriously. "I think you may have to scrub floors on your knees. They spend a lot of time on their knees, Catholics do. Praying and confessing."

Praying, she could do, but confessing. Now that was something else entirely. "I won't go. Maybe we could run away. Go to our ranch and live there, just you and me."

"That would be fun, wouldn't it?"

All that afternoon they played at what it would be like to live on the ranch, the two of them. Alone and together, for always.

"But we won't get to go there, will we?" Edna asked that night, the very last night she would spend with Lena Jo.

"No, probably not. But we'll never forget each other and we'll love each other all our lives."

"Oh, Lena Jo," Edna cried. "I can't bear to leave you and the little log school and James and all our friends. What will become of our ranch and Major and the mules and sheep? I'm afraid none of us will ever come back."

"Oh, you will. I'm sure." Lena Jo didn't look like she believed what she said.

They slept in each other's arms all night.

On the train, Mother looked so sad Edna tried to hide her own confusion. She wanted to be with Mother and Daddy, but they should be going home to the ranch, not off to some faraway place where, for all she knew, Daddy had died. She dried her tears and sat prim and straight, like a lady. In spite of all she did to be good, Mother continued to look faraway lonely. Before too long, her fear turned to worry about Daddy.

The silence was about to kill her. "You'd tell me if Daddy was dead, wouldn't you?"

Mother turned to stare down at her, a stricken look on her face. The train rattled and swayed and hot sunlight poured through the dirty window onto her lap. Mother remained so still she could hear her own heart throbbing painfully. He was dead! That's why Mother came to get her.

Huge, racking sobs grew in her chest and she tried to hug them tight enough they couldn't escape. Out they came anyway, and her stomach turned over.

Suddenly her mother's arm was around her, pulling her close. "Hush, child, hush. Your father is not dead. We want you close to us, that's all. He'll be in the hospital longer than we'd thought, and it's time you were near us again. We are a family."

Torn between her love for Mother and Daddy and the friends and life she'd left behind, Edna continued to cry. Though relieved that Daddy was alive, she couldn't seem to stop. After a while, Mother grew angry.

"Hush that, now. You're not a baby. Stop acting like one."

And so she did, but it didn't stop the ache, not one bit.

Seeing St. Mary's and Sister Josephine for the first time convinced her she would never be happy again.

The taxi picked them up at the train station and dropped them off in front of a large, white frame house. She could hardly bear the wait after Mother's knock stopped echoing.

The door swung open and inside stood a woman who looked much like a crow, all dressed in black with wings rippling to rest at her sides. Her round face peered from a black and white frame.

"Yes?"

Mother introduced herself, an arm around Edna's shoulders like she might sense her need to run away. Far, far away.

"Ah, yes, indeed. And this is little Edna, is it?" The eyes, round and black like a bird's, darted in her direction.

She was never going to be happy again. This was not a place she wanted to be. She clasped Mother's dress like a baby, which was indeed how she felt, a helpless baby who could do nothing about what was about to happen to her.

Mother put down Edna's valise, turned to her and gave her a hug, then moved from her embrace. "Now you go with Sister, Edna, and I'll come get you this weekend so you can see your father."

Through narrowed eyes, she studied her mother, and the lie written in her expression. Daddy was dead and this was where she would stay. Forever. And she'd be forced to become a nun, give up men, and spend her life on her knees.

"Hurry up, child, don't dally so," Sister Josephine said, and swept along the hallway of the sprawling structure, her wings fluttering out at her sides.

Numbly, she lugged her bag and followed the woman in black, who did not look the least bit happy to be loving God. She kept her gaze on the long black skirt that swayed back and forth as the sister walked. She didn't look back. If she did, Mother's lies would have left her face and the truth would be there.

Like she always said, if you lie, everyone will know. Well, she didn't want to know Mother was lying.

If Daddy was dead, she'd stay in this place all her life, serving God. It shamed her that she didn't want to do that.

She was only there a day before she knew that the place was worse than she'd imagined, much worse. Boring lessons, boring work, ugly rooms, boring food. No, worse than boring food. Disgusting food.

Willing to give it one more chance, she hoped for better the following day, but nothing changed. On the third morning, she sat at the breakfast table with twenty other girls and stared into the same slimy bowl of oatmeal as yesterday and the day before. Except for one thing. They got thin milk one day, sugar the next, then back to milk. Never both at the same time, though it would have done little good.

Perhaps what they didn't eat was poured back into the pot to be serve the next day.

Around her, everyone stuck their spoons in and began to eat. Though she already knew how it would taste, she tried to do the same. Gagged before her lips closed around the spoon. Were they doomed to eat this every morning? It would seem so. She'd probably starve to death, and one day they would find her on the hard cot in the room she shared with five other girls. Cold and stiff and blue, her ribs sticking out.

Next to her, Loretta, the girl who slept on a cot next to her, whispered, "Better eat it."

"It's awful."

"Shhh," Loretta said.

At that very moment, a ruler smacked down on Edna's shoulder. Hard. "Hush. No talking at meals. Eat."

She bit her lip and swallowed the slime. Even while it slid down her throat, she imagined it coming back up. She'd spew it out all over Sister Katherine, wielder of the ruler. The idea amused her and allowed her to finish eating.

No laughing, though. No laughing at the table. Fine, who'd want to laugh anyway?

Over those first few days, Loretta, who was twelve and had been at the boarding school most of her life, tried to teach her how to get along at St. Mary's.

"The sisters are all from Ireland and England. They are very strict and we must follow all their rules of good behavior or be punished."

"When do we get to play?" Tedda asked.

"Oh, we don't. We have one free hour a day after supper, and it's for reading."

"Well, I do like to read. What kind of books? May we have our own?"

"You'll probably get the Bobbsey Twins because you're so young."

"That's for sissies," Edna said. "I'll get some of my daddy's books."

"I wouldn't if I were you." Loretta rolled her eyes. "If you get caught, you'll really be in trouble."

"Then I won't get caught."

Mother came to get her on Saturday to take her to see Daddy. She still didn't believe he was alive until they joined him under the shade of a verandah attached to a large building at the place called Ft. Bayard.

Daddy sat in a big wooden chair with wheels on either side and he had a brightly colored blanket over his legs.

"There's my Edna," he said and smiled. Not at all like himself. But alive. Oh, yes, alive.

Joy filled her up like warm sunshine. He wasn't dead, but his eyes had dark circles around them and his face was much thinner than it had been. She could hardly bear not to rush to him and throw herself into his arms.

Mother had already warned her she must not hug Daddy or get near him because TB was catching. So she stood back, hands clasped behind her back.

"Hi, Daddy. How are you?" Being so formal and distant from him made her heart hurt.

"I'm better, much better. Soon I'll be out of here."

She swallowed painfully. "Good, then you can come get me from that terrible place and take me home."

"Edna," Mother scolded.

"It's all right, Cassie. Let the child be. She needs to say how she feels." He looked back at her. "It won't be long now—" He choked and a spasm of coughing bent him forward. He coughed until she feared he would stop breathing.

Cassie went to him and put a hand on his back. Edna wanted to run across the dusty courtyard, run so far away she could no longer hear the terrible sounds coming from her father. Mother had touched him, what if she took the terrible TB too?

"Darling, it's all right. Daddy's fine," Mother said.

After a while he stopped coughing, and they were able to visit some more before they had to leave to catch the train back north to the cage from which she could never escape.

Staring out the window of the train at the arid, empty desert, she decided she didn't like this part of New Mexico much. It wasn't like the high desert with its crisp air and brilliant sunlight that cast shades of golds, oranges, browns and lavenders over the land; that lit the frosted mountains with purples and blues that painted a frame around the valley.

She was so sick for home her chest ached and she thought she might die, which wouldn't be such a bad thing. Surely heaven wouldn't be like St. Mary's.

And that horrid place just kept getting worse.

One terrible day, Sister Josephine, who had taught Edna her catechism, stood at the front of the class, ruler at hand and announced in a big, loud voice:

"Easter Sunday, Edna Smith will celebrate her First Communion. She will attend confession with the rest of you on Saturday afternoon."

Everyone stared at her. They wanted to laugh, but dared not.

"Confess?" she squeaked aloud. Surely they wouldn't expect her to confess? She hadn't done anything bad to confess.

She wasn't aware that she had blurted out the question until she saw Sister Josephine's glare.

"Yes, what is it, Edna?"

She lowered her lashes to cover her shame. "Nothing, Sister."

In bed that night she told Loretta about her problem.

"I don't know what to say. I can't think of a single solitary thing to confess."

"Well, it's like having bad thoughts. Surely you've had some of those. We all do."

Thinking hard, she could come up with nothing she would want to tell a priest. All her bad thoughts were directed at the nuns and this place. He surely wouldn't forgive those. And telling them might get her another hard swat with the ruler. Anyway, how did you tell someone about your inside secrets? Those were only to share with friends. And her friends were back home, not here. Even Loretta, who had helped her, wasn't her friend. She was too prissy.

The next day she found a Zane Grey book while cleaning rooms, and she stuck it under her dress. That evening she propped the hated Bobbsey Twins up in front of her and hid the Zane Grey inside. What exciting stories she found there, about living on ranches and riding horses and chasing bad men.

The ruler came down with a whack on her shoulder, startling her from her fantasy world. Sister Josephine stood behind her, one hand held out. Without a word, she closed Zane Grey and handed it over.

The very next morning when she was completing her daily chore of dusting the stair bannister and the parlor, her mind began to wander back to the pages of the exciting western story. As she went down the stairs, she flipped the dust rag here and there. Flip, flip, flip.

"Dust every day, dust every day," she muttered. How could anything be dusty every day?

"Edna," came the firm tone she'd grown to know so well. "That's no way to dust. Go back up there and do it right this time."

Frowning, she trod upstairs and started over, the sister standing at the bottom of the steps, arms folded over her skinny bird chest. When Edna reached her, she tossed the dust cloth down on a table and turned to face Sister Josephine. Jaw jutted, she stared up at her.

"Put that cloth where it belongs, young lady."

"Where does it belong?" Tears slipped out. She'd be late to class and get in trouble again.

The sister took her hand, shoved it down on the cloth, closed her fingers, then marched her to the cleaning closet. "Put it in there, and remember the next time to do your job right, young lady."

The nun sashayed away, skirts swinging from side to side.

Still crying, Edna raced up the stairs muttering under her breath, "Goddamn Sister Josephine, goddamn Sister Josephine anyhow."

She didn't realized she'd spoken aloud until one of the older students came out of a room and laughed. "Well, now, Edna. I guess you'll have something to confess Saturday."

In her room that night, she threw herself onto her cot. "I won't," she cried to Loretta. "I'll run away first. I won't confess. Grandmother always washed my mouth out with soap for swearing. Why couldn't Sister do that instead?" Terror stricken at the idea of having to confess her horrible sin to a priest, she cried most of the night and by morning had made herself sick.

Mother came to get her that weekend, and she vowed as they rode the train to Ft. Bayard that she would run away where they would never find her. She would never go back to St. Mary's.

"Auntie Alice is coming by to visit on her way home from California," Mother told her when they were settled in the car. "It will be so good to see her."

Edna barely acknowledged her. She wasn't sure she remembered Aunt Alice.

Cassie brushed the child's hair back from her face and put a finger under her chin. "What's wrong? You look ill."

Tears poured down her cheeks, but she didn't say anything, just gazed at Cassie with misery.

Cassie's heart lurched. In her attempt to deal with her own problems and Finas' illness, she had ignored her poor little girl. Crooning, she took her in her arms.

"Oh, I'm so sorry. I know this is hard on you, being apart from us...from your daddy." How could she tell her he was dying? There was simply no way. She had to be protected. Time enough when it was all over.

Her own tears flowed as she held her precious daughter.

Later that day she and Alice sat together on the verandah while nearby Edna huddled miserably watching her father sleep in his chair in the sunshine.

"She doesn't belong in a convent, Cassie. You know she doesn't," Alice said.

"It's not a convent." Cassie wiped her eyes. "Oh, Alice, I don't know what to do. I always thought I was strong, but this..." she gestured with her white handkerchief. "I'm falling apart. She's so unhappy, but I need to do what's best for her, and Finas needs me now so badly."

"I'll take her with me," Alice said, in a tone that said that settled it.

"Oh, I couldn't...I mean...how could you?"

"Rose. She can stay with Rose. You know how our sister is. The more the merrier. She'll be with family. Everyone all around to care for her, see to her needs. Plenty of cousins to play with. You won't have to worry a minute about her."

"I know that, but..." she glanced at Finas, then at her suffering daughter, who had refused to tell her why she'd cried all the way from St. Mary's to Ft. Bayard.

Alice lay a hand on her arm. "Honey, you have enough to worry about. We'll see Mama Cooney doesn't get too harsh with her discipline. We'll all love her. That's what's important now."

"I know." Cassie sighed. So far away. Casselton, North Dakota. Yet what a wonderful place to grow up, with so many loving aunts and uncles and cousins and her grandparents. Perhaps it was for the best.

"When are you going?"

"Tomorrow. We'll be home in time for Easter."

Cassie covered her eyes with the handkerchief and cried. How she wished she could be home for Easter, amidst the loving arms of her sisters and her parents. At the moment, she felt as if she needed their tender reassurance as much as her daughter did.

Alice put an arm around her. "There, there. You must be strong for your Kentucky cowboy. I know how much you love him, and he you. Be strong, and let us worry about your child for just a little while."

Cassie nodded and dried her eyes.

Alice stood. "I'll talk to her, if you'd like."

"Yes, please. I can't, not right now. I'm afraid she'll see her father's...uhm...oh, God, Alice. Is his death written on my face? I want to hope, but..."

Alice hugged Cassie for a long while without saying anything, then went to speak to her niece.

And so Edna missed her dreaded confession, but she vowed never to swear at another person again. As it turned out Aunt Rose taught her the catechism, but she never made her first communion. She went to live in North Dakota with the Cooney family. She would not return to New Mexico for more than two years.

During the first weeks on Cooney Island, the great shadow of her father's certain death haunted Edna. Everyone in the large family was too kind to her, and that made her believe all the more that she would never see him again.

Not all of the family lived in Casselton, but they were all near enough to visit frequently. Aunt Margaret, the oldest, lived near Enderlain, Aunt Mary lived in Breckenridge, Aunt Rose in Sheldon. That left Aunt Sarah and Aunt Alice and Uncle Jack in Casselton. There were fifteen cousins in all, several about her age. Soon she became the pet of the family, embraced in loving arms. But there were times, oh, yes there were, when she felt anything but treasured.

It never occurred to her that they pitied her mother until she reinstated the fine art of eavesdropping, and heard much more than she wanted to know.

"The child curses in Spanish, I just know those words aren't civilized," one of the aunts remarked as they sat around the parlor sipping tea and acting like some kind of fancy ladies.

At this, Edna smothered a giggle. She'd been showing off for the cousins, saying things like gato, chango, diablo. They did sound like bad words. More so than the milder com esta, y muy bien and gracias. Practically all the words she had learned from Mexicans while at the Perkins' house.

She went back to listening through the half-open door.

"Well, what do you expect? Our poor Cassie marrying that…oh, dear, you don't suppose he might be part Mexican, and she's ashamed to tell us."

The question sounded as if it came from behind a cupped hand.

"Don't be ridiculous."

That was Aunt Alice, the one she loved most of all the aunts. All the way from Silver City to Casselton she'd held her and spoken softly, running her fingers through Edna's hair. She hadn't cried all the way, but felt like someone was squeezing her heart to make it stop beating. Aunt Alice helped make the feeling not quite so bad. She was the best.

"I've met the man, and he is not Mexican," Aunt Alice said. "though I'm not sure there would be anything wrong if he were."

A loud gasp from all as if they were one. "Why, Alice," Grandmother rebuked.

"Oh, Mother, don't be so Victorian. This is 1923, after all."

Edna strained to hear more. Surely if Daddy had died the aunts would know it and discuss it. She lived in fear of him dying and no one telling her.

She nearly jumped out of her clothes when the door suddenly swung open, and there stood Aunt Rose. "Child, what are you up to?"

"Uh...nothing. I dropped something."

"Oh, Edna. Don't you know it's not proper to eavesdrop? We're going to have to work on your manners. You're a Cooney girl and you must act like one."

"No, I'm not. I'm a Smith girl." Edna set her jaw and glared at Aunt Rose.

"Children don't speak to adults like that." Aunt Rose looked worried rather than angry, and she softened her rebuke by smoothing Edna's hair. Taking her hand, she led her away from the parlor and the gathering of adults.

"Your Aunt Alice has told me of the troubles you had at St. Mary's, and we've decided to send you to public school. I can teach you your catechism, and then we'll ask Father O'Reilly to give you your first Holy Communion."

The pronouncement eased Edna's fears somewhat, though she worried about the deadly confession.

"Well, how do you feel about that?" Rose asked.

"Fine."

"Say, fine, Aunt Rose. Or fine, Ma'am."

"Yes. Okay."

Aunt Rose sighed.

There would be a lot for her to learn, but Edna wasn't so much worried about that as not knowing about her father.

Cooney Island was only an island in the spring when the rains filled up the coulee, but all the cousins liked the sound of the name, and so it became that to Edna as she made her way carefully into their lives. All the girls were as beautiful as their mothers and very ladylike, while Edna preferred to wrestle and play with the boys, but soon learned that wasn't allowed.

"We're not even allowed to go in the water till we can swim," Aunt Rose's daughter Dorothy quipped.

"But how can we learn to swim without going in the water?"

"That's the idea, silly. That's exactly it."

Dorothy laughed and took Edna's hand. She was three years older, and the leader of the younger three girls who were all within six months of each other. "Come on, there's plenty of fun to be had. I'll show you."

Out under the big shade trees, the four cousins sat while Margaret educated them. "We're supposed to believe the stork brings babies, but let me tell you…"

Margaret's dad was a Frenchman and very proper, but he taught his daughter the things of which Aunt Rose would never speak. Much of Edna's sex education came from there and she learned such things as flirting was permissible as long as it was carefully controlled.

"Young men should never put their hand on your knee," Margaret said with a shake of her dark curls.

And so Edna was indoctrinated into the Victorian world of the large family. Summer was a time of great fun, with as many as eight to ten cousins gathered at Cooney Island most of the time. They ate apart from the adults, the girls were not allowed to wear makeup or high heels. She wasn't sure what the boys were or weren't allowed to do, they seemed free to be absolute idiots most of the time.

Much to their dismay, they never quite made a lady out of Edna. Perhaps she had too much of her Kentucky cowboy father in her, plus a pride of self and a determination to be her own woman.

It was in sixth grade that she fell in love with reading everything from Kipling to the fine print on soup labels. She especially liked Greek fables and Western novels, and saw nothing unusual about that.

She came to enjoy living in Casselton surrounded by loving aunts and uncles, grandparents and cousins. And she resigned herself to never seeing her father again, though some nights she continued to cry herself to sleep.

Chapter Seven

Cassie's Journal—1924

Today, after four months on the job, I resigned from my nursing position and went to work for the Red Cross. I think I'll like it much better.

As a nurse, I had hoped to learn more about this dreaded lung disease once called consumption. This terrible tuberculosis. Even the most learned of doctors can only prescribe rest, fresh air and sunshine. I expected to find a magic pill, and when I didn't, felt totally helpless.

Our life has become one long journey through a world of illness and imminent death.

By some miracle Finas began to improve in spite of all dire pronouncements to the contrary. Hours spent lying or sitting on the sun porch taking the air appeared to be healing him. As he grew stronger, Cassie began to fantasize about joining Edna in North Dakota when he mended. They could have a good life there, far away from this hateful desert.

Physiotherapy helped him along the way to mending, and his interest grew in taking part in life once more. He progressed enough to have a weekend off occasionally. To her delight they joined other couples to travel away from the hospital. Digging for relics became one of his favorite pastimes. She was more than pleased to go with him in any endeavor that removed them from the confines of the hospital.

One morning she arrived at the hospital to find him sitting at a table in the sunroom looking over a newspaper. His cheeks had taken on some color, his thick hair gleamed. The change had come about so gradually she hadn't noticed, but he looked and acted so much healthier. Did she dare believe he would truly get well and they could go home? She kissed him on the cheek and sat down. How wonderful to pretend they were at their own breakfast table like a normal couple.

"What're you reading?"

"I'm thinking of buying some land." He glanced at her quickly, gauging her reaction, she supposed. "To replace what we lost."

Speechless, Cassie clutched her throat with one hand and tried to appear enthusiastic while her hopes and dreams of building a new life away from New Mexico slipped away. Her promise to follow her husband anywhere if only God would let him live nagged at her.

He continued as if he could dispel her arguments if he talked fast enough. "We can sell that 640 acres back to the government for twenty-five cents an acre and use the money to buy a better place."

He continued to speak in glowing terms of this land, but the buzzing in her head muted most of the words. Bits and pieces drifted into her consciousness.

"...water...the Tusas River runs through it...there's a house too...a thousand feet higher..." Whatever else he may have said became a mass of indistinguishable words. It was still the desert, vast and remote and lonely.

Finally, he paused and glanced at her. "Well, say something. Aren't you happy I'm getting out of here...going home?"

"Home?" she asked in a whisper. "I have no home."

And then she lifted her head to meet the expectant gaze of his brown eyes, sparkling like they had when she first met him. A love for this man, so deep and abiding, filled her to overflowing. To have him healthy and happy meant more than her dream of living with the Cooneys. How childish of her to want to run home to her parents. She was a grown woman, this man's wife, mother of his child.

Sometimes, we have to weigh the things that make up our lives. We have to realize that it is love that brings the most happiness. And we must face that we don't always know what to do. We just have to listen to the spirit that lives within us. Settling for something we thought we did not want at all, can often be the thing that makes us happiest.

That revelation hit her as if spoken from her inner being, even as she gazed at him, at the naked hope on his face. She swallowed her disappointment, bitter as it was. Besides, she'd never be content to live the way her sisters and brothers did.

How badly she wanted there to be another solution for them besides that damnable desert. But it wasn't to be. She had, after all, made a promise. God had kept his part of the bargain and made Finas well again. Now she had to keep hers, and what's more, do it happily and with grace.

Swallowing thickly, she took his hand. "Tell me about the house," she said in a trembling voice.

Words tumbled one upon the other. "Well, it's log. Better than a tar-paper shack. Supposed to be a big old place. It's on 240 acres, but we'll buy more as we can. It's a very pretty country for both ranching and farming. Did I tell you it's a thousand feet higher than Taos Junction?"

This meant little to her, but his enthusiasm was catching, and seeing him so full of plans for their future filled her with hope that somehow she could come to love this place like he did. While her head told her to beware, she vowed to make this work.

Settled on the train, Cassie sat in silence next to Finas, who took the window seat because he wanted to watch the country go by. He'd been penned up for so long in the hospital, he must feel like he'd been freed from prison.

It was a long trip by train from Silver City, with several changes and layovers before they would reach Tres Piedras, and she worried the strain would be too much for him. Though he slept off and on, he remained vigorous and eager throughout the trip.

It was late March, and winter refused to release its grip on the sagebrush flats of Northern New Mexico. The train passed between high banks of snow, taking them to their new life.

At Tres Piedras they emerged from the heated car into a brisk, sunny day. Finas took a deep breath and she held her own, waiting for the dreaded cough to strike. It didn't, and he put a hand on his chest to feel it rise and fall.

Then he turned to her, wrapped her up in his arms and began to laugh. She sensed if he'd been stronger he would have lifted her off her feet and waltzed around on the depot dock. Without hesitation, she joined his mood of gaiety, ignoring the stares from others gathered at the small station.

Soon enough, these folks would grow accustomed to Finas Smith and his shenanigans.

After a while he released her and gestured toward the three huge boulders above the town. "Three Rocks. Tres Piedras. Home."

"Home," she repeated, and closed her eyes in a silent plea. *You promised, now make it work.*

The dilapidated log cabin hadn't been lived in for several years and would need a lot of work, but it was large. It sat on a rise in a high mountain valley ribboned by the rambling Tusas River. In the front yard Cassie stood next to Finas and gazed out across the rolling pastureland interrupted occasionally by long exclamations of pine and spruce. Amidst walls of vivid green, patches of golden aspen reached pale bare fingers toward a brilliant blue sky. The river, no more than a few feet wide, tumbled madly with early snow melt. By North Dakota standards, it wasn't much more than a stream.

The cold air tasted and smelled crisp and tangy.

"God, isn't it beautiful?" he said, and put an arm around her waist.

"Yes. Yes, it is." And lonely…empty. Nothing, no one, for miles. But it's okay, it's going to be okay. *I'll make this work, I will.*

She shivered in the stillness.

"Cold?"

"Um. Let's go inside."

On the way, he stooped to gather an armload of wood from a stack alongside the porch.

"Where did that come from?"

"Over that rise. Plenty of dead fall in the woods."

"No, I mean, how did it get here?"

"Oh, I talked to McCowan, storekeeper in town. Asked him to hire someone to cut us some wood. We'll have to put on a hand or two, at least for the spring and summer months. We can use the pension money to pay their wages. It'll be just about enough, what with boarding them. He tells me some of the fellas who gave up their homesteads near the junction will be glad for work."

Cassie spared him a glance. After his initial disappointment over the loss of everything on the old homestead, he'd never spoken of it again. It seemed such a waste, those two years they'd labored so hard only to have it destroyed. Stock, house, furniture, all gone. But they'd never had much to start with, had they?

By spring thaw on the Tusas River, they'd had enough of the drafty log cabin and began plans to build their own home. She liked the look of logs, and so, with the help of a couple of fellas desperate for work, they put up a three-room log cabin, fairly large with a beautiful fireplace. There were plenty of bookcases to hold his large collection, and Navajo rugs for the shiny pine board floors, and local Tewa pottery.

And the piano. Such a glorious addition to their home. She and Florida McCowan had shopped the second-hand stores in Antonito and Alamosa until each found the instrument they wanted. Florida bought a player piano so she could use it at the dances if no musicians showed up.

Though Finas had taken some convincing, he'd finally given in and paid $50 for a used piano. With the addition of a Delco light plant they had electricity and, joy of joys, a well on the enclosed back porch. No more hauling water and bathing in a wash basin.

There wasn't much cash to be had and anyone with a steady income, such as his pension and disability check, was considered well-off. Somehow that pleased her. It was difficult to escape the influence of her upbringing.

On a golden afternoon in August of that first summer at Tusas, she sat to rest on the front porch and gazed out over their land. The aroma of rough-sawn timbers mixed with the fragrance of wild flowers and moist soil from the river bank. The mules, Jake and Jack, grazed with several horses on the desert grass, alongside a few head of cattle. Finas was talking of buying sheep. There were chickens in a pen and late beans and squash and pumpkin waiting in the garden. If only they could bring Edna home and be a complete family again, everything would be perfect. She'd be at peace with the world. How she missed the child, with her bright inquisitive eyes and dear expressions.

Then Finas came home from town a few days later, his expression one she knew only too well. Something was up, and she probably wouldn't like it. She awaited his announcement with dread and anticipation.

"I'm thinking of going up to Cumbres and working for the railroad this winter. There's a job come open for the season. You ought to go with me. We can certainly use the cash."

One deep breath and she didn't think she could take another. When she did it was all she could do to maintain a normal tone.

"What on earth for?" Fists clenched at her sides to keep from yelling, she awaited an explanation.

"Now don't get in a tizzy. It's only temporary and, like I said, we could use the money."

"Here I thought we were doing very well. We have some stock, a good team of mules, some machinery. I've got my chickens, a dog and our cats. And a Chevrolet passenger car. The house is perfect. I was going to talk to you about going after Edna before winter so we could all be together. Here, in our home." Tears filled her eyes and she shook her head angrily. Men. Always stirring things up just when a woman got herself settled in.

"Aw, honey. Much as I'd like to see her, I think we ought to wait till spring. The money will help build up the ranch, and besides, winters are tough out here."

"Well, then, Finas Smith, what are we doing with this place if it's too tough to live here but half the year?"

He shrugged, looked helpless for a minute, then took another tack. "It'll just be this first winter. After I work this fella's job while he goes to Arizona, we'll come back. We'll buy more stock and machinery, we need to build a bunkhouse. Once we add to the stock, we'll need to hire more help."

"And what about the stock we have? And our house. Do we just let everything go like before? Lose everything? Come back here to nothing? I can't…I won't start over again. Please." She hadn't meant to cry, but the tears spilled over anyway. She removed her glasses and wiped them away angrily.

His arm snaked around her. "Aw, now don't you do that. We won't lose a thing. We'll get someone to live out here and take care of everything."

"And what'll that cost? Everything you make at Cumbres?" She hunched her shoulders, pulled from his embrace and steadied herself, glaring up at him. "I'll stay here. I can take care of things." The offer did not come easily, and she regretted it immediately.

"Oh, no. I couldn't have that. No. Huh-uh."

"You don't have a say in the matter, Finas Smith. None at all. If I want to stay, I will. Even after I was grown, my dad dictated my every move. He kept me from becoming a nurse until we married. For that matter, he almost kept me from marrying you. Right now, I'm not sure but what he wasn't right about that. But, so help me, you'll not do the same. I'm not your child. Besides, it'll be fun."

"Fun? When the snow covers up the windows and doors and you can't get out. And you're all alone?"

"I'll dig my way out. Besides I'll have the animals for company. We can lay in a good supply of food."

"And how will you get around? To town for supplies and the like?"

"Well, I imagine old Bill and I can manage quite well. You taught me to ride for a reason, though I always suspected it was to keep me from crawling behind the wheel of our new car once I taught you to drive."

"You had a wreck in your old Model T, you well know that's the reason I forbid you to drive again. I don't want you hurt. Besides—"

She held up a hand. "Okay, fine. Let's stick to the point."

"The point being you aren't a rancher, you're a woman."

87

He might as well have set a fire under her. "I am not leaving this place. Now if you think you want to physically carry me away, I guess you can do that. But I wouldn't advise it. Not if you want to come back to a happy home. I'm half of this marriage, this ranch is our home and I'll carry my weight, same as you. I didn't sit in that hospital with you for two years to have you tell me I'm only a woman and not able to do my part."

He didn't want to give up. She could see that in his eyes and the set of his mouth. But when he spoke, she knew she'd struck a nerve.

"I'll always be grateful that you came out here with me, Cassie. I know you didn't want to. And I'm grateful you stuck with me while I was so sick. If you're set on doing this I can't change your mind, so I guess I'll have to give you my blessing, but only provided the Naylors can get you a telephone put in out here. If anything happens, you're to call for help immediately. I'll get someone to check on you once in a while too, and there'll be no argument about this."

She allowed him a tiny smile and a nod.

He ran a hand through his hair and shook his head. "Sometimes you're a true wonderment to me. I never thought you'd be happy here, figured you'd be eager to go off somewhere nursing at the first chance, and now you're refusing to leave."

"Well, that just goes to show you." All her nerves fluttered with insecurity, but he would never know that, not in a million years.

"I reckon it does," he said with a wide grin. "Now, come here."

She went into his arms, heart beating fast and hard. What had she gotten herself into? How would she ever last out the winter alone here? After she'd fought so hard to get her way, she wasn't sure it was what she wanted to do at all, but she wasn't about to back down.

That winter there were times—at least a dozen a day—when she wished she had gone with Finas. But then she'd sit near the window, a warm fire at her back and watch the morning sun burst over the Sangre de Cristos, turning them blood red. Watch the snow blanket across the valley glistening like someone had tossed buckets of diamonds over the land; gaze at the unending sky as it flashed from purple to lavender to gold to cerulean blue. Then she'd know for certain why her husband loved this place, why she herself was learning to do the same.

That didn't ease the difficulty of handling everything on her own. The daily struggle through the deep snow to put out feed for the animals, the woolen scarf wrapped around her mouth and nose growing stiff as her breath froze in its folds. Her glasses fogged over until she couldn't see each time she entered the warm house, the frigid cold that reached deep into her lungs like tiny knives. She often wondered how this could possibly be good for a person. Any person, not just one with TB.

A thousand times she wondered what would happen if she fell in the deep snow and couldn't get back to the house to use the telephone the Naylors had arranged to have installed.

On good days, she liked to walk the mile and a half to the post office in Tusas and visit with Mr. Gallegos. When the snow was deep, that distance might as well have equaled the miles to the moon, for she could not get out and no one could get in. She could stand being penned up only so long, then she would saddle old Bill, and wrapped so thickly she could hardly mount, ride for an hour or more, just to get out of the house.

Mrs. Naylor came to see her one sunny day in late November, just appeared on the porch, stomped ice and snow off her boots at the door and knocked. She'd never met the woman and was nearly bowled over by the strength of her appearance.

She was long and lean with skin like fine leather and thick, graying hair cropped short and stuffed under a floppy hat. She wore a dark woolen outfit with a split skirt for riding, and was bundled in what appeared to be a man's overcoat with high topped masculine boots on her feet.

"Name's Nancy Jane Naylor. Husband's Harry, ranger in Tres Piedras. I couldn't stand the thought of you out here all by yourself." The hearty voice matched her looks to a tee. "Times when my Harry goes off into the mountains that I about go crazy. He lit out this morning and I thought of you. Figured we might commiserate a while."

And commiserate they did. Before long Cassie found herself sharing even the most intimate of details about her upbringing and her feelings about living in New Mexico.

Nancy looked around the immaculate cabin, her glance lingering on Finas' collection of books and magazines.

"For someone who is here against her will, you seem to have settled in. I don't know many women who'd agree to spend the winter out here alone. Especially not a city girl with your background." Her steel gray eyes bored into Cassie's.

A bit miffed at the remark, Cassie replied, "I don't take my marriage or responsibilities lightly."

"Of course you don't. Neither do I. Finas seems a fine man. Kentucky born and bred, like myself." A wide smile revealed strong teeth.

"He is that." Cassie stopped short of sharing details of her personal life with this stranger. She had a way of prying even the most private details out of her, so she quickly changed the subject.

"Would you like some coffee? I keep a pot on the back of the stove. Or I could brew us some tea."

"Ah, a good cup of coffee would do me fine. And now tell me how you are getting along here on your own."

Cassie balanced the glass dome of the percolator with a finger while she poured a cup of steaming black coffee. "Well, it's not too bad, really. I have the radio. And books. And plenty of supplies. Everything is rigged up in case I get snowed in completely, which I understand may happen soon."

"Oh, indeed it will. You can bank on that."

"Cream, sugar?"

"No, straight up is fine."

After pouring herself a cup of tea, Cassie settled back on the sofa beside her guest and took a sip before going on. "I have 200 pounds of flour, 100 pounds of sugar, 200 pounds of potatoes and 50 pounds of onions. Oh, and plenty of coffee and tea. Milk comes from the cow, and there's Bill, of course."

Nancy raised an eyebrow and looked around with a confused expression. "Bill?"

Cassie laughed. "Our horse."

Their combined merriment filled the room.

"Then there's Maisie and Gwendolyn. My cats. They're in on the bed. And I do enjoy the piano."

"How nice that you play. It must be good company." After another sip, Nancy again pinned her with that steely stare. "And nights you're scared out of your mind and you probably cry from loneliness for another human. Especially that Finas of yours."

Cassie nodded her head. "How could you know?"

"Because, I've felt the same more times than I can count. Living with men who love this desert enough to live on it is a trying experience."

"Thank you," Cassie murmured, and hid her trembling lips with a raised cup.

"Whatever for?"

"For making me feel better about not being stronger."

"Well, I've noticed that folks who put on a brave front often make those of us not so brave feel guilty. Revealing one's shortcomings often eases other folk's burden. Underneath we aren't so different, us humans."

Batting away tears, Cassie asked, "How long have you been here? You and your husband."

"Oh, a good long while. We came up before the war. He was already a bit too old to go off fighting a young man's war. He liked the outdoors and so being a ranger suited him fine."

"And you? What do you do?"

"Keep him a warm hearth and clean home, be a mother to his daughter. Nell Frances. She's near the same age as your girl. A bit younger." She rubbed at her woolen-covered knee. Finishing off her coffee, she stared out the window, like maybe she thought she should have done more.

Not sure what to say, Cassie let the silence settle around them. It was clear that this woman knew a lot about her and Finas, probably from him visiting with her husband in town. That made her feel a bit jealous of the time she wasn't with him.

91

"And what about you?"

The woman's sudden question startled her. "Me?"

"Finas tells us you were a nurse. That's a fine profession. How can you...just give it up?"

Cassie picked at the embroidered pillow. "It wasn't easy, but..." She shrugged and let go the subject.

"You have a daughter. You must miss her very much. Will she be joining you soon?"

"Oh, yes. In fact, as soon as spring breaks, I'll be going after her. She's with my family in North Dakota."

Nancy nodded. "My Nell will be glad to have the company."

The crackling of pine burning in the fireplace broke the comfortable silence that rested around them.

The realization that this woman would become a good friend left Cassie with a serene feeling.

Chapter Eight

Edna's Diary—North Dakota,1925

I really don't care if I take First Holy Communion Easter Sunday. It's not my fault. Being a Catholic isn't what it's made out to be anyway. I never even heard of it in Servilleta. And if being like Sister Josephine is what being a Catholic means, then I'll just pass, thank you.

"So how come you can't take communion?" Roberta asked.

Edna tossed her head, raised her chin and stared at her cousins, her three best friends. "Dumb old priest said because I went to public school I couldn't participate. I don't care. It's stupid, anyway. I think I'd rather be an atheist."

Roberta gasped and shuddered. "You don't mean that. Then you'll go straight to hell, no ands, ifs or buts."

Margaret and Dorothy stared in disbelief.

"Nah, I don't believe that stuff. I think if I'm a good person and never hurt anyone, or treat them mean, then I can go to heaven."

"But atheists don't believe in heaven."

Edna planted both hands on her hips. "That doesn't mean there isn't one."

Roberta shook her head. Dorothy and Margaret, who had stayed out of the discussion, spoke up.

"I personally don't care if you're an atheist," Dorothy said. "It's rather brave."

"Me either," echoed Margaret. "We're still the four one-and-onlies. No matter where we go or what we do, or even what we believe in, that'll always be true."

Edna nodded with the others. Their friendship pact, made soon after she arrived in North Dakota, couldn't be broken by such a dumb thing as whether she took first communion or not. More than the Cooney name, or even the Catholic religion, bound them together, and it sure couldn't tear them apart. Nothing ever would.

Since they were only twelve, except for Edna who hadn't had her birthday yet, the girls ate with the young ones at their grandparents' home. You had to be fifteen to sit at the table with the adults, a rule that caused the four girls to roll their eyes every time a meal was served at Grandmother's house.

Easter was the next day and they were all going to Mass together. One huge Cooney entourage would represent the descendants of the founders of Casselton. Only Edna would remain sitting in a pew with the younger ones while everyone else went forward to take communion.

Soon after supper, while the girls gathered in one bedroom to compare and admire their Easter dresses, a car rattled to a stop outside.

"Wonder who that is." Edna was the first to jump up and hurry to the window.

Her breath fogged the glass as she leaned against it to peer down. In the drive a woman crawled out of a taxi and the driver unloaded a small suitcase for her. With the bag in hand he followed her toward the door and out of sight.

"Who is it?" Margaret asked, crowding Edna.

"I can't tell. It's some woman."

The words had no more than left her lips than Aunt Alice called from downstairs. "Edna, come down. Come down right away. Hurry."

She did just that, feet scarcely touching the steps, her cousins close behind. There, standing in the foyer, stood her mother, peering through her round glasses up the staircase at the girls, puzzled, as if she didn't recognize her own child. She had removed her coat and wore a familiar navy and white dress.

"Mother," Edna shouted, bounded down the steps and flung her arms about her startled mother's waist.

"Oh, Baby. My goodness. You've grown so big." She pushed her out at arm's length and studied her with shimmering eyes. "I didn't imagine you'd be all grown up. Look at you. You're so pretty."

Edna squirmed. Big was okay, in fact growing bigger was terrific, but Grandmother Cooney never allowed people to tell the girls they were pretty. Said it went to their heads.

"What did you think, that I'd be a baby all my life?"

Mother laughed and Edna did too, then hugged her again. Mother was really here, but what could that mean? Daddy was well, she'd had letters.

"Are we going home?" Torn between the desire to be with her parents and the fear of never seeing her best friends again, she dreaded the answer, whatever it might be.

"It's about time, don't you think?"

Grandmother Cooney had remained in the background, hands clasped over her ample stomach. Now she stepped forward.

"Let your mother go, child. She's had a long trip." Putting an arm around her daughter, she steered her into the parlor. "Come and sit down, tell us what's been going on. Is he still set on remaining in that uncivilized country?"

Edna and the one-and-onlies crowded close. Grandmother Cooney never called Daddy by his name, insisted on referring to him as he.

"We have a lovely home, Mother." Cassie submitted to her mother's ministrations as she was seated in the love seat upholstered in creamy material with tiny wine colored flowers. The girls hung back. This was probably an adult moment, and Grandmother would send them from the room shortly.

"I can only imagine," Grandmother Cooney said.

Unable to contain her excitement, Edna said, "Will I have a room of my own? And do we have horses? Is the new place as nice as the old?" The questions poured out before either adult could stop her. Given the chance, they would have. Especially Grandmother, who believed children were meant to remain silent and out of sight, if at all possible. And she could see it was possible.

"Child, child. Leave your mother be. Let her relax a moment. There'll be time later for all your questions."

Mother gave Edna a look of understanding and touched her hand. "We'll talk later. Perhaps you and I can share a room for the night and we can catch up."

Grandmother glowered at her daughter, then at her granddaughter but did not object, though it was clear she wished to. No one in the family was ever sure how to react to Mother since she'd run off and married a Kentucky cowboy.

As Edna and her cousins reluctantly left the room, she heard Grandmother Cooney say, "I just don't understand how you could possibly have lived all alone in that godforsaken place for the winter. Or worse, why in the world you let him talk you into it."

Before the door closed fully, Edna heard a portion of her mother's reply. "I'm not a little girl, Mother. No one tells me what to do—" and the rest was cut off.

Clearly, Mother would take no sass from Grandmother. Edna grinned. Maybe she'd tell Grandmother to stop calling Daddy he while she was at it.

Much as she wanted to return home to New Mexico, Edna dreaded leaving Margaret and Roberta and Dorothy. Would the one-and-onlies ever get back together again? It was such a long way to New Mexico, and she dreaded the trip though she so wanted to go home.

Some time later a tap on the bedroom door sent her heart leaping about in her chest. She could hardly contain her excitement when she opened the door and let her mother in. A new life was beginning for her, she felt it in her bones. At last she and Mother and Daddy would be at home on the ranch. At last she would have a normal life, and not be shifted around from one place to another.

At the train depot Aunt Alice hugged her. "Write often."

Then there was Aunt Rose, who added, "Take care of yourself, child."

Grandmother held first Edna, then her own daughter close. "You know you can come home if you need to."

"All aboard, all aboard," called the conductor.

The train hissed and tooted, the bell rang. The sun shined warm on her cheeks.

Edna struggled to tear away from the cluster of cousins, kissed Margaret and Dorothy and Roberta each in turn. Mother took her arm and tugged her away from the noisy group.

"Come on, child. We have to board."

Goodbyes filled the air till nothing else could be heard, save the rumble and hiss of the steam engine.

Teary-eyed, Edna stumbled up the steps and into the passenger car. On her knees at the window she waved and called goodbye. The train lurched forward, steam spewing a thick fog so she could make out only ghostly forms.

"Goodbye, goodbye." The window muted their shouts of farewell.

When the station disappeared out of sight, she turned and sat in the seat beside Mother, tears rolling down her cheeks. She didn't mean to cry, she really didn't. It just kept happening like the tears might never stop.

She wore a light blue traveling dress made by Aunt Rose for one of the cousins. It was tight and itched under her arms.

Mother touched her knee. "Darling, I know you will miss the girls, but I have a very good friend and she has a daughter near your age. Nell Frances has been dying for you to come home so she might have some company. I'm sure you'll get along super. You'll see, it'll be all right. And you do want to be with Dad and I again, don't you?"

Ashamed, Edna rubbed the tears away with the tips of her fingers. "Oh, yes. Yes, I do. It's just that I'll miss the one-and-onlies so very much."

Mother arched a brow. "Yes, well, I know you'll like Nell Frances."

If she's not a crock. She didn't voice the thought aloud. Mother might not appreciate slang. They had been a long time apart, and it would take awhile before she learned her new boundaries. With Grandmother there was never any doubt where the lines were drawn.

She and the one-and-onlies knew what to keep to themselves. But she had been a mere child when she left home and couldn't remember what was allowed and what wasn't. She certainly hoped she would be able to speak her own mind, like with Aunt Alice, the very best aunt in all the world. The only adult who agreed that Edna was nearly grown.

Instead of testing the limitations just yet, she glanced at Mother and smiled. "Tell me about the ranch. Is it pretty?"

"I wrote you all about it."

"I know, but I want to hear you say the words. I want to see it in my head. What was it like spending the winter alone there? I wish I could have been with you. Were you frightened?"

Cassie smiled and patted her daughter's hand, leaned back against the headrest and told her about her adventuresome winter alone at Tusas. Though she had written some of it in letters, she found herself going into much greater detail.

"By Christmas the snow was deep, the wind had blown a drift over the windows at the back of the house so I could only see out the front. I had plenty of wood stacked in our bedroom. Your dad had them pile it up till I couldn't get to the bed, and so I slept in the front room beside the fire. The log walls are thick and chinked so it was not too bad cold if I wore plenty of clothes.

"From the front porch I could see the river and the elk came down early of a morning to drink while the sky was still pink and lavender. They'd dip their dark hairy muzzles into the cold river and lift their heads to look around. Water running off their chins caught the light and made sparkly little rainbows. On clear days the sky looked like spun candy before the sun came up. Then it turned an ice-blue so brittle it might have cracked wide open at the touch.

"I remember when I was a girl walking to Mass on Christmas Eve in Casselton. The snow would crunch under our boots and our breath would billow out in great clouds."

Edna nodded, felt a connection, for she had experienced the same thing in North Dakota.

"Up at Tusas it gets so cold that the snow underfoot is hard as ice and squeaks when you walk on it. And you dare not uncover your mouth lest your lips and lungs freeze solid."

This made Edna laugh and Cassie joined her, knowing she was exaggerating a bit. But not much.

No, not much.

"When I went out to feed the animals, the woolen scarf I wore across my mouth would freeze stiff from my breath. In the utter stillness of dawn, the mules and horse and sheep would be all crowded together, like the best of friends. White billowed from their nostrils to hang over them like clouds.

"And sometimes I was so lonely I'd snuggle in their warm midst, lean against old Bill's shoulder and carry on conversations with them. I was afraid to cry for fear my tears would freeze on my cheeks. In the house I sometimes carried one of the cats around talking to her just to hear the sound of my own voice. Or I'd play the piano. It was a life-saver."

She didn't go on for a moment, remembering the days when she'd craved the sound of another human voice so badly she'd pick up the phone and call the Naylors just to hear them talk. Often she'd cried into her bed pillow far into the night. But these were things best kept to herself. No one, least of all this child or her father, ever need know that. Or that she was often terrified of the utter isolation. She scarcely admitted that, even to herself. The very vastness of the desert had frightened her. As if it might open up and swallow her, leaving not a trace she'd ever existed.

"Well, you won't have to do that again, will you? I'll be there, and if Daddy needs to go away, we'll handle it together. I'll be company for you. And we can play duets."

"Oh, that's right. You took lessons from old Mrs....?" Cassie stared in disbelief at this child who'd turned from a mere babe to a half-grown woman while she wasn't looking, and marveled that she and Finas had produced such a lovely, dark-haired sprite. Edna might look like her, but Cassie saw Finas in nearly every move she made. That stubborn set of her jaw, the brown eyes that probed so sharply she oft times felt her brain tickle.

"Tell me more. I can almost see it when you talk."

Cassie nodded and gazed out the window. So could she. Drawing a deep breath, she went on with her tale.

"Then the worst weather would pass and we'd have a break from the brutal cold. The sun would shine so brightly I couldn't look out the window at the snow cover for fear of being struck blind. And the air, oh, glory, how sweet and crisp it would be. I'd sit on the porch just breathing deeply for the sheer joy of it.

"Decorated by snow the juniper and pine on the mountainsides shimmered like thousands of Christmas trees, their scent filling the air. Old Bill and I made the rounds pretty well. The Tusas post office and store are only a mile and a half from the ranch. I liked to walk for the mail except when it was stormy or the snow was too deep. Mail is delivered on horseback to the post office there by a man named Sanchez. Mr. Gallegos runs the store and the post office which is in the store."

Enraptured, Edna gazed at her. Cassie wasn't sure she even knew this lovely person sitting beside her, but it was so good to be with her. So sorrowful to have missed so much of her growing up.

"The Naylors are the forest rangers at Tres Piedras, and as soon as they heard I was going to stay alone, they had a phone put in. I would call them every day so they would know I was okay. She's from the same part of Kentucky as your Dad, but she's older. We've become close friends.

"The McCowans run the store and hotel in Tres Piedras. Florida is a case, I tell you, but we are good friends as well. She's meeting us at the train station to take us home." She patted Edna's hand and went on with her story.

"They...the McCowans...were likewise interested in my welfare, so I wasn't out of the world. There'd be letters from you and your aunts and your father. Several of your father's magazines to read when I got home, and I had a radio. When I went for the mail I would visit with everyone. Someone always mentioned how brave they thought I was for staying out there alone through the winter. That would nourish me all the way home.

"I'll tell you a secret, if you'll keep it always."

Edna nodded, eyes bright and wide.

"When your father told me he'd bought the ranch, I was so disappointed. Knew I would hate it. But this winter, alone there with only the animals, the mountains and the river and the sky as companions, I fell under its spell completely. The fragrance of sage brush when it blooms in early spring, the rush of the river when the snows melt, the magnificence of the mountains. The way the warmth comes sneaking in when you least expect it to chase away the bitter cold. It humbled me, made me so thankful that I was allowed to share something so supreme, so breathtaking."

She ruffled Edna's hair, reveled at the way the girl regarded her, admiration in her dark eyes.

"I'll love it too, always. Even when I'm old. And I'll never have to go away again."

Cassie laughed and hugged her child. Life overflowed with joy. Alone through the long winter at Tusas she had discovered inner strengths she'd not known she possessed. Her husband was well and happy. Her daughter was beautiful and smart. And she was content and happy. They would all be together at last. At Tusas.

Chapter Nine

Edna's Diary—1925

Last night Daddy gave me a box he made for me while he was in the hospital. My treasures went in the box—a gold bracelet, a beautiful handkerchief, my Indian gloves, my letters from best friends. I will keep it forever.

It reminded me of another time when I was small. My grandmother in Kentucky used to keep the visiting church missionaries who came at least twice a year to the Methodist church in Clay. Most of the ladies were well trained in entertaining children. I was always glad when Miss Cora came. She was large and dark. She wove wonderful stories for me and showed me many small tricks.

One day she took a matchbox and pasted small pieces of wall paper on it and made it beautiful—to me. She put a small handkerchief, three beautiful glass beads and a wooden spoon, the kind we ate ice cream with then, in the box and gave it to me. "Here is your treasure box," she said. I was five. That box stayed with me until I was eight and then I lost it.

When I think of leaving behind all my friends, my cousins, I feel like sometimes I am losing the things I need most to remember...like I lost my little box.

But this one from Daddy...it I will keep the rest of my life.

Eager and excited, Edna craned her neck to catch a first glimpse of home through the car window. Mother and her friend Florida McCowan jabbered on, but she really didn't listen.

The car put-putted along the narrow, crooked road, gears whining as it struggled up the steep hill, leaving behind the three towering boulder formations for which Tres Piedras was named. In the driver's seat Florida chattered and maneuvered the muddy ruts expertly. She'd have to be careful and not refer to Mrs. McCowan by her first name aloud, but what a fab name it was. Not at all ordinary like her own.

They climbed through masses of pine that flowed down to ring the valley below. Remnants of snow clung to the north slopes with a stubborn tenacity.

Farther along the incline, a car meeting them slithered into a drive-out to give them the right of way. Mother waved at the people staring out the open windows. Florida only shouted hello and kept her broad hands firmly latched to the jittery steering wheel.

The rugged ruts led them higher along the rim of a mountain valley, cut by the narrow, shimmering ribbon of a meandering river. Excitement built in Edna's chest until she could scarcely breathe or speak. Almost home. So beautiful. So breathtaking.

"Look, Edna. Down there. That's the ranch."

Nose pressed tightly to the window she stared far down at a log cabin that looked like a dollhouse. Florida executed a turn and maneuvered the car along the sloping lane. To get a better look, Edna pulled herself forward by the back of the seat, sat back down, stood again.

"Darling, please sit still. We'll be there soon enough." The smile on Mother's lips gentled the words.

Before they came to a complete stop in front of the house, Edna wrenched open the back door and piled out to clatter up the porch steps and bound inside.

Daddy met her midway across the room and lifted her high, as if she were still that nine-year-old who had left him for dead in a hospital so long ago. She clamped her arms around his neck and held on tight. Laughing, he begged her to release him so he could breathe. Then he whirled her once, twice, three times, both of them shouting with glee.

"Finas Smith," Mother said from the doorway in her stern voice.

Looking contrite, he released his daughter. "Yes, dear?"

The tone of innocence set them all to laughing. And then Mother was hugging him.

"Will you never grow up?" she whispered, before stepping back.

"I certainly hope not." Then he turned to Edna. "Well, did you have a good trip home? What do you think of the place? Are you ready to put on britches and be a ranch hand?" He tilted his head at her. "They didn't turn you into a dude up there in North Dakota, did they?"

At each question, she opened her mouth to reply, but then he asked the next without waiting. By the time he stopped asking, she didn't know which one to answer.

"Well?" He arched a brow.

She gazed into his brown eyes, so like her own. "I hope not. But Grandmother did her best to make a lady out of me." She paused, her glance sliding over books lining shelves on three walls and the piano. How happy Mother must be to have it.

"Oh, I'll bet she did. Tell me, are you a Cooney girl now? All proper and lady like?" Amusement drew lines around his mouth.

"Not really, I'm afraid."

Again everyone laughed, including Florida, who hovered in the doorway, holding two satchels and regarding the family with open fondness.

Cassie took note of her friend. "Oh, Florida, let me have those. Edna, run out to the car and get the rest of our things. Oh, my, I'm tired, and certainly pleased to be home."

"And I'm glad to have you here, both of you," Finas said, and held out his arms to his girls.

After Daddy released her, Edna ran to the car and fetched the rest of the luggage. Halfway back to the house she paused and gazed around at the wooden corral fences and outbuildings. In the meadow several horses grazed. She took a deep breath and smelled new lumber and aromatic pinon, wet earth and pungent sage.

Though she could not know what the future held for her, she vowed that no matter where she went this place would always be home. Bursting with happiness, she ran to the house, Mother's valise banging against her leg.

Early the next morning, she dressed and hurried into the roomy kitchen off the great room. The smell of bacon and coffee sweet in the air. Mother stood at the wood-burning cook stove, her face flushed. Daddy was at the dry sink, staring out the window, hands stuffed in his pockets. The long table was set with three places at one end. Goodness, there was room for many more, and signs that others had already eaten and left.

She had a feeling she had interrupted something between her parents, but both turned to greet her with wide smiles, and she let it go. No time to make trouble where there was none.

"Good morning, sleepy head. Everyone else has had breakfast and gone to work. Were you going to stay in bed all day?"

From Daddy's tone she knew he was teasing and grinned with a happiness that filled her to the brim. Tomorrow she would eat with the ranch hands Mother had written her about. Texas cowboys, they were.

"You aren't going riding in that dress, are you?" Daddy moved to sit in one of the chairs, and Mother placed a platter of bacon and eggs in front of him.

"I...uh, riding? Today? Really?"

She brushed at the knee-length dress Aunt Rose had made for her, following the latest style, then glanced from Mother to Daddy. Both nodded, and he pulled her chair out to reveal a parcel wrapped in brown paper.

"Your mother got your measurements from Aunt Rose and we ordered you some britches from the Sears & Roebuck catalog, so you can be a ranch hand." He certainly was proud of himself, seemed about to bust with it.

Mother's feelings weren't so easily read.

Edna grabbed the package and ripped it open. Inside were three pair of stiff new jeans pants. She held up a pair, the legs dragging on the floor.

"You can roll them up till you get your full growth," Mother said, turning to take a pan of biscuits from the oven. "It seems you're a bit shorter than the size that fits you everywhere else."

"Oh, they're perfect. Perfect. Thank you so much."

"Sit, child. Let's eat."

An impossible task that, but she did her best to cram a few bites into her mouth, though her mind had fled outside to sit astride a horse, to gallop across the flats, the wind in her hair.

After breakfast, she stuck her legs in the stiff new britches, hopping from one leg to the other for fear Daddy might get tired of waiting for her. In her heart she felt much as she had the time Daddy had taken her riding on the homestead the very day after they arrived, a vivid memory she would never forget. Except this time she would have a horse of her own and make a new memory. Her hands fairly trembled rolling up the pant legs and stuffing her feet in her shoes. Maybe she'd get a pair of boots soon.

After a lesson in saddling Tony, the stout little quarter horse she'd picked from the herd, she listened to Daddy's riding instructions closely.

"Sit easy, weight in your stirrups, don't jerk the bit in his mouth, but let him know who's boss right off. You're in charge and don't neither of you forget it." Then he gave her a boost up and she was actually sitting her horse.

The saddle felt comfortable as a rocking chair, and she waited with anticipation while Daddy adjusted the stirrups. After a brief lesson on reining, Daddy mounted and heeled his own horse, a long-legged roan named Micky, into a trot, and they were off. Tony easily kept up with the larger horse, and she soon settled into the rhythmic movement of his gait.

In all her wildest imaginings she'd never believed she would have her own horse to ride. Of course, she'd dreamed and wished, but dreams and wishes had a way of not coming true.

"Well?" Daddy asked after they'd ridden for a while. "What do you think of the place?"

"I love it."

"Yes, me too. Today I'll show you pretty much all our land. We're starting with 240 acres, not near what we had on the homestead, but there's water and grass. I hope to buy more land soon." He reined in, stood in the stirrups and pointed toward a square adobe house in the distance. "That's the Sewells' place. They have a daughter named Enza. You'll get to know them soon."

"What about the Naylors? Mother said they have a girl my age."

"Well, actually she's almost a year younger than you. Nell Frances is her name. Her dad, Harry Naylor, is the forest ranger over at Tres Piedras, and his wife is Nancy. You'll meet lots of folks. Summer is when everything happens. Parties, ball games, church doings. Makes up for being snowed in for six months each winter."

"What about school?" This was a question she hadn't wanted to ask Mother, but thought it safe to ask Daddy. Though she dreaded to hear the words, she had to know if they were going to send her away once winter came.

"We'll not worry about that now. There's time later to make plans. I…we, want you to have a great summer."

Well, he hadn't exactly promised, but it would have to do.

He studied her with glistening eyes. "It's good to have you home, girl. Real good."

A knot grew in her throat. She'd never felt the closeness between herself and her parents that she'd yearned for. Daddy had always been away, first at war, than in the hospital. And Mother gone off as well. In her mind, though, she loved them both as they loved her. It was just hard to speak aloud of such things.

Before she could reply to his words, he kicked Micky into a gallop and she did the same with Tony, following him across the valley toward the border of green trees. The spring sun shone hot on her back and the wind smelled fresh as a newborn day. Joy filled her from the very tips of her toes to the top of her head. It felt as if her body was shining brighter than the sun.

Over the next few months, she often rode or walked the valley from one end to the other. Much of the extra grazing pasture was free range forest land. There were few fences and plenty of space to get lost in. Except for the cattle and sheep, she was alone with her thoughts and the book she always carried tucked into a saddle bag.

True to his word, Daddy gave her chores to do, but they were not difficult and she mostly enjoyed them. Care and feeding of the horses fell to her, which she enjoyed. Once, when one of the hands had to be away with his sick wife, she kept care of the sheep. That wasn't a difficult job, though occasionally, she would become immersed in a particularly exciting Zane Grey story and end up having to search for the herd when it wandered off to better grazing.

That penchant for reading developed another bond between her and Daddy and she gleefully waded through his vast collection of Zane Grey. In the evenings, they would have endless discussions about a particular tale and why it had enthralled them both. He bought books and magazines and newspapers for entertainment, like other men bought whiskey and beer. And he said it often, too.

Because of his health, hired hands were needed year-round to keep the ranch functioning. Of course, more in the summer. They did all the heavy work, like clearing sagebrush for more grassland, or killing the prairie dogs that chewed the ground full of holes into which a horse could easily stumble and break his leg. She learned that Tusas meant prairie dog. It didn't take her long to see that both the nearby settlement of Tusas with its store and post office, and the river of the same name were aptly named. The pesky critters were everywhere, and it was a constant battle to keep them under control.

Daddy was supervising the building of a bunkhouse. Most of the help were World War One veterans who had come to New Mexico to claim the 640 acre homesteads. Most too, had failed to prove up those waterless acreages. Many had left but some had remained and needed work. All but two of the hands were unmarried and had no place to live, so if they were going to work on the ranch, there needed to be a bunkhouse where they could sleep.

Mother fed them and Edna was expected to help with that as well. However, much of the time she found herself free to roam. And roam she did. No twelve-year-old ever spent such a wonderful summer.

For her birthday, July 11, when she actually turned twelve, Mother and Daddy invited the surrounding families for a party. Everyone brought food and one of the homestead men brought a lovely decorated cake.

Mother took it reverently and set it as the centerpiece for the large table they'd carried outside.

"However in the world did you do this?" she asked of the blushing rancher.

He leaned close, and Edna had to strain to hear his explanation. She knew only too well how Mother and Mae had struggled to bake cakes in the high altitude and had never succeeded.

"Well, to tell you the truth, Mrs. Smith, Henry and I got together and we just kept baking cakes till we got two layers come out pretty good, then we put them together with lots of melted candy bars for icing. Took us a good part of a day."

Mother stared hard at him for a long moment, then began to laugh. She laughed so hard that everyone gathered around to join her. Nothing would do but that he tell the story over again so they could all hear.

The party was a huge success and Edna received a pair of riding boots that Daddy had ordered from a catalog. They were a bit roomy, but she thought them perfect.

"I took your shoes and drew around them, then told them to send half a size larger so you could grow a bit."

Edna gazed at the shiny black boots, tapped her feet several times, then with tears in her eyes, looked up at Daddy. "This is the first time I ever hoped I wouldn't grow much more."

This brought another round of laughter. Everyone laughed a lot that day, and it seemed nothing in the world could ever go wrong again. She played the piano and everyone sang and then Mother played to more singing. It was a wonderful day. Edna was careful, however, to cross her fingers.

One evening a few weeks later, while she and Daddy sat reading and Mother embroidered a pillow slip, a horse approached. Curious, Edna ran to the front porch and watched the rider dismount, tie the reins to the hitch rail and start to the house.

"Hello, young lady. Your dad at home?" He regarded her with sparkling eyes, his face tanned so that she knew he must be a rancher. "Tell him Ford Bradley's come to see him."

"Daddy," Edna called, but before she could go inside, her father stood at the door.

"Well, howdy. What brings you out this way?"

The two men met in the yard and shook hands. "I was headed for Taos and the wife asked me to stop by to remind you that there's a dance at the school house Saturday night. We were thinking you might want to come. You and your wife and daughter."

"Well, now, I don't know," Daddy said.

Edna clasped her hands over her stomach and held her breath. She wanted to ask Daddy if they could go, but didn't know how he would take that in front of this stranger. Yet, she so wanted to go. It would be a perfect chance for her to visit again with all the boys and girls her own age who had come to her party.

As if reading her mind, Mr. Bradley said, "The wife thought maybe it would be a good time for the young'uns to get together again. I know it's hard on them to be alone. I reckon near everyone will be there."

Daddy swung a gaze in her direction, his lips curling at the corners. She couldn't help herself, she nodded and held her hands under her chin in supplication.

"Well, I reckon if Cassie wants, I might take the two of them over. I myself am not much for dancing, but don't see any harm in it. Why don't you come on in? It's nearly dark. You can spend the night in our bunk house, and be on your way come morning. I think we could even wrestle you up a bite of supper."

Bradley lifted his hat and turned it a couple of times in broad fingers. "I thank you kindly. I just might take you up on that, seeing as how you might not charge me too much. Reckon it'd save me putting up in Long John's road ranch."

"Neighbor don't charge neighbor," Daddy muttered, then said something under his breath she couldn't hear.

Bradley chuckled. "Well, you gotta admit the man's got money savvy."

"And a monopoly on road travel. Imagine having to pay to cross a bridge. The man's greedy. He don't have to own everything, but looks like he does."

The two men stomped into the house, but Edna remained outside for a while, watching stars blink to life in the silvery sky. Long John

Dunn was often a source of conversation around the house and at the store in Tusas. She'd once heard him referred to as Juan Largo de Taos, and wondered what that might mean. For sure, Daddy didn't like him, but Mother spoke of him with respect. Mother liked everyone, and Daddy sometimes accused her of being too trusting, but she'd just laugh and shrug.

Would the rich and famous John Dunn attend the dance Saturday night? How exciting to get a chance to see her friends again. What would she wear?

Come Saturday night at the school house in Tres Piedras, Long John Dunn was nowhere to be seen, but the building was filled to capacity. Edna would never remember everyone's name. She teamed up right away with Nell Frances, who had been to the house with her mother a couple of times since the birthday party. She liked Nell a lot. Heads together, they compared the boys they'd like to dance with.

"I think Mrs. Sewell's brother is keen," Nell said into Edna's ear.

"Leonard? I don't know. What about that boy there, who is he?" Edna indicated a lean, dark-haired boy who strutted around the room looking tough.

"Oh, you don't want mixed up with the likes of him. That's Joe Miller. His dad's a bootlegger."

Miller? The same family who wouldn't let their children get shots? Her best friend back in second grade at Taos Station was Jane and her little sister June had died of typhoid fever. The idea that the Millers were bootleggers sent chills running down Edna's spine. She'd probably been too little to understand at the time. And this Joe? Was he the sullen eighth grader she remembered? Sure a lot better looking now than then.

She tugged on Nell's arm. "That's so exciting. No wonder he didn't get invited to my party. A bootlegger. Mmm."

"The whole family is tough. There, that's their mother." Nell pointed at a tall, bony woman with a harsh look, graying hair pulled into a bun so tight it stretched her skin. Dressed plainly, she stood apart from the other women who watched the younger set dance to music from an old piano in the corner.

It wasn't long before boys were lined up to dance with Edna and Nell. She danced the two-step waltz with a boy named Johnny, then swirled into the arms of another boy for a lively foxtrot polka. The entire evening flew by in a blur of laughter and dancing, and she only saw Nell briefly. What a wonderful evening, and how much fun to have the boys so eager to take her whirling round and about the floor. During the evening Edna searched for Jane Miller, but never saw her.

The music played on into the night. Some of the men got polluted and fell asleep in various poses without causing any trouble.

Several sets of square-dancing ended the evening, and she wondered as she locked arms with Nell, if she looked as sparkly and self-satisfied as her friend.

At the end of the final dance, Daddy came and fetched her. "Time to go. Mother's waiting."

They walked outside toward the Chevrolet, with boisterous good nights echoing into the night.

"See you in the morning for Sunday school," someone shouted.

"Well, what did you think of that party?" Daddy asked when they were settled in the Chevrolet.

Edna smiled. "It was fun. More fun than we ever had in North Dakota."

"Oh, I'm sure." Daddy laughed and started the car.

After Sunday school the next morning, held in the same room as the Saturday night dance, Florida McCowan greeted Cassie and Finas and Edna, obviously bursting with a piece of news.

"What's tickled your funny bone?" Daddy asked.

"You're not going to believe this. Last night, after the dance, some of us were hanging around talking, and here comes that fanatic old Mrs. Duffing carrying a bucket of soapy water."

"Come to mop the floor? That time of night?" Mother asked. "Well, isn't she ambitious."

Florida started to laugh again, and took awhile to get control of herself. Before long she had everyone within earshot laughing along, and eager to hear her story.

"It seems she…well, she doesn't agree with all our sinful dancing and carrying on."

"Oh, my," Mother said. "What did she do?"

"Before anyone could stop her, she had taken a scrub brush to that piano and washed it inside and out with that soapy water. Ruined it, I'm sure. A shame too, considering how much it will cost to replace it."

"I wondered why we didn't have piano music at the service. Why did she do that?"

"Said she wanted to scrub the devil out after the dance Saturday night. That poor piano wouldn't play a note this morning. It may never recover."

Edna wasn't sure how funny the story was, but just listening to everyone laugh, she couldn't help but join in. Still, how could anyone think the devil was in a piano? She did know, however, that music and dancing were thought to be a sin by some.

"I think maybe if Grandma had been there, she might have done the very same thing," she said.

Daddy and Mother and Florida laughed harder than ever.

That fall they rented a drafty old barn of a house in Tres Piedras so Edna could attend school there. In a way she was relieved they would all be together, but she sure had hoped they could stay on the ranch all winter.

On the first day of school, Miss Langley, who taught the four upper grades, ran through attendance, asking what grade each one was in. Edna was the only one in seventh grade. Nell was eleven months younger than her, so was ready for sixth.

"Hmm," Miss Langley said, tapping a pencil against her teeth. "How many eighth graders?" A few hands went up. "Okay, Edna, then you'll be in eighth grade too."

Mother wasn't as excited as she was at skipping a grade, which meant only one thing to Edna. She would finish school sooner and get to live at Tusas year round.

"You'll have to work extra hard," Mother said.

"She reads well, though, Cassie, and we can help her," Daddy said. "You'll work hard, won't you?" He ruffled her hair and smiled.

Happy to have him on her side, she quickly agreed. "Oh, yes. Yes, I will."

Because of the size of the big old log house they'd rented, they were chosen to board the two teachers for the winter, which Edna wasn't sure she liked. It made her feel like she had to study or pretend to do so all the time. That was baloney, but she didn't say so aloud.

But that's what attracted all the cowboys. They came and went all winter, sticking around to eat, visit and play cards, but mostly to vie for the attention of the new schoolteachers.

The hijinks of the courting cowboys almost made up for the discomfort of being under Miss Langley's watchful eye.

Miss Langley, who was barely eighteen and pretty as a picture, was from Kansas. And she knew nothing about the West. Edna thought she was sort of show-offy, talking all the time about what a wonderful adventure it was to live so primitively. Edna couldn't wait till she was eighteen and could come and go as she pleased. Then no one would ever keep her from living at Tusas all the time.

Miss Durham…Mother called her a straight-laced old maid…was from Missouri and really old. Twenty-six, at least. Some of the cowboys weren't too picky, or maybe they thought they stood a better chance with an old maid. Anyway, both ladies received a fair amount of attention from the lovesick men.

Edna enjoyed sneaking around and spying on the goofs. Miss Langley finally narrowed her choices down and picked herself a "hero." Dressed to the nines, boots shined, sandy hair parted in the middle and slicked down, and smelling to high heaven, he would come courting. As far as Edna was concerned, he'd be better looking in a cowboy hat astride a horse, the wind blowing the stink out of his greasy hair.

Hero would get all nervous when in the teacher's presence, and it was soon evident that he was in love. All lanky six-foot-three of him. About the time that became apparent, he brought along his brother, shorter, darker and much better looking.

The old maid Miss Durham soon took to following him about, but he was more interested in playing cards than in her.

Mother remarked once that the both those boys might as well not get too serious, as she knew their mother, and she would have no part in either of them marrying a girl who couldn't even milk a cow.

The situation was fun to watch, considering there wasn't much else to do but go to school and help keep the drafty old house clean. The lovesick shenanigans and reading everything she could lay hands on were what got her through the year without going crazy.

One day Edna learned just how hard times were. Mother sent her to the store. She gave her a dollar to buy a can of red salmon and some soda crackers to make salmon cakes for supper.

"Now, honey. You'll get thirty-five cents change," she explained. "Don't lose it."

"I won't." It perturbed her a bit that Mother would think she couldn't be trusted to bring home the change.

From the shelves of Mr. McCowan's store, Edna picked up a can of red salmon and moved along the aisle, staring at the offerings. Her gaze lit on a jar of sweet gherkin pickles, the picture on the label showing a girl holding up one of the delicacies.

Oh, my, how she wanted one of those tasty pickles. Mother and Daddy would like those with the salmon cakes, she was sure. Her mouth watered at the thought of such a treat. Marked on the top was twenty-five cents. She could do arithmetic pretty well, and figured after thinking about it a minute, that she would still have change left if she bought the pickles. For a long time she stood with her fingers around the jar, then picked it up and took it and the can of salmon up front where she asked for soda crackers, which Mr. McCowan kept behind the counter.

He wrapped her purchases, and showed his white teeth in a large smile. "That'll be ninety cents, Edna."

She handed him the dollar and held out her hand for the dime in change. She'd been right, there was still change left from the dollar.

"Say hello to your mother and father," he said.

"I will," she said, and skipped outside.

When she ran into the house Mother turned and smiled at her. She took the sack and opened it before Edna could tell her about the pickles.

Standing in the center of the kitchen, dime clutched in her hand, Edna stared up into her mother's fury.

"What did you do? Where did this come from?" She held up the jar and stared at Edna in a way she had never done before.

Edna opened her mouth to answer, but Mother looked at the price on the jar and her voice grew louder. "Twenty-five cents? For pickles? What were you thinking?"

"I brought back change," she said, and opened her hand to show the shiny dime in the palm.

Mother grabbed it. "Well, that's good. A dime. What am I going to do with that?"

"Mother...I'm sorry...I thought."

"No, you didn't. You didn't think at all."

Mother turned her back, fists clenched at her sides. Her shoulders began to shake. "Go on, go play. Now."

Nothing more was said of the incident, but Mother didn't put the jar of pickles on the table for supper, nor for any meals for the next week or more.

Edna never knew if she told her father, he never said a word about it, but the following Sunday a week later, when Mother sat them on the table, he opened the jar and smiled.

"Well, well. A special treat. How nice."

Mother stared at her plate and said nothing.

One thing was for sure. Edna never wanted to make Mother that angry again.

At last it came time to go home to Tusas for the summer. Miss Langley and Miss Durham went back to their respective homes in Kansas and Missouri, leaving broken hearts strewn all around.

Chapter Ten

This summer has been the happiest of my entire life. Long rides over the hills and valleys. Parties and church picnics and Saturday night dances at Tres Piedras. We girls have the boys held in the palms of our hands. They wait in line, eager to have a dance with each of us.

Often we stay on the ranch two or three weeks at a time, but we are not without company. Strangers and neighbors alike stop by, some spend the night. Others for an evening of singing. The boys tell tall tales about the war and they play cards in the bunkhouse at night. We can hear them laughing and hollering at each other when we sit on the porch and watch the stars come out.

I suppose this is a hard life, as Mother often says, but the beauty and serenity make up for it in so many ways. My heart will be here always.

Edna stared with despair at Mother. "High school in Durango? In Colorado?" Her voice raised an octave and she struggled to control it before continuing. "After I finished eighth grade in Tres Piedras, I thought I could live on the ranch and help Daddy. I'm grown up now."

"Well, perhaps you think you are, but you have to have an education. And you can't get it here. You'll finish school in Durango and spend your summers here."

Scowling, Edna stared down at the floor. "I don't want to go away from Tusas and you and Daddy, too. It isn't fair."

"It's not like you're going all alone. Dad will stay on the ranch, I'm going to nurse at the hospital up there. We'll stay with the Marrs. You remember them, don't you?"

Edna wiped her eyes and stared out the window at her beloved Tusas ranch. She wouldn't go. She'd run away, come home and once she was here and the snows were deep Daddy would have to let her stay.

"Edna, you do remember Mae Marr, don't you?"

She nodded. "Of course. But doesn't it count what I want to do?" Tears nearly choked her.

"Children don't run the family, adults do."

"I'm not a child, I don't want…" She couldn't continue.

"We don't always get what we want. Nell is leaving too. In fact, the Naylors are moving away so she can go to school."

"And that makes it all the harder. Losing my best friend and my home, all at once."

"You're not losing either. Life is moving on for you. Please don't make this so difficult. Prove you're an adult and face this head on. We will go to Durango, and that's all there is to that."

A sob caught in her throat and she swallowed it. She nodded miserably and turned to stare out the window through her tears.

"Well, then." Mother stood as if that settled it.

And of course, it did.

Edna spent the following week riding the valley alone. Taking first Tony, then Old Bill, then Micky and finally Beauty, she memorized every foot of her beloved land. To each of the horses in turn, she bid goodbye, promised she'd see them in the spring, and walked back to the house.

The day before they were to leave, she went alone to stand on a rise gazing in all directions while umber shadows trailed the sun across ochre and green pastures; watched the Sangre de Cristos flame blood red in the dying light, as red as they'd once been when seen by the Spaniards who'd settled this land and named them "Blood of Christ Mountains."

Sick at heart, she whispered goodbye, then turned and trudged back to the house in the gathering dusk, not turning her head one way or the other. Everything was branded in her mind, and she'd carry it all with her, for always.

A week later she and Nell fell into each other's arms and wept their farewells, then she and Mother bid Daddy goodbye and boarded the train for Durango.

Enduring school was not something Edna was good at. She studied and received decent grades. Not to do so could mean repeating some courses and delaying graduation. If she worked hard she could graduate sooner and go home to stay.

Meanwhile, the summers spent at Tusas would keep her from losing hope altogether. And summer did indeed finally come.

That year Mother began to have parties at the ranch, admittedly as much to entertain herself as her daughter. Nearly every weekend, a group of youngsters spent time there. One of their favorite sports was tennis. It didn't take a fancy court, a flat grassy place did just fine. They played cards and went riding and had picnics and hiked all over the countryside.

The fun days would be topped off with homemade ice cream and cake and singing around the piano.

When it came time to return to Durango, Edna went with less reluctance. There was always the following summer to look forward to. Being a sophomore was no easier than being a freshman had been. Neither was making friends. If she had to sit out at dances, as she often did, she would remind herself how popular and in demand she was at the dances in Tres Piedras. There the boys lined up to dance with her and the other girls.

She was so homesick she couldn't bear to think of the time when she'd have to come back. Finally, she made it through the term and returned to Tusas determined to talk Mother and Daddy into letting her stay out of school a year. If she did, she could take some extra courses and graduate in her junior year before she turned seventeen. That seemed a good argument to present to her parents, who wrote how much they missed her.

Back at home once more on the ranch there was often a surprise or two to liven things up.

Everyone around Tres Piedras knew Mother was a nurse. Because Doctor Martin lived and worked in Taos, and there were no others closer, she might be called upon to stitch someone's wound or tend a fever or soothe a belly ache that wouldn't go away.

Soon after Edna's return, as the family settled down to sleep one night, a car rattled into the yard and someone started yelling and honking the horn.

Daddy relit the lamp and grumbled his way into pants and a shirt while a fist hammered on the door, a voice shouted for help.

Mother told Edna to stay in the back room and dressed quickly while Daddy went to the door and let in two men, one being supported by the other because he could barely walk. Wide-eyed, Edna watched from the darkness of her room.

"Mrs. Smith, you gotta help him. He cut his leg the other day, and we been trying to take care of it, but it looks bad, real bad. Can you do something for him?"

The excited young man was Luke Jefferson, one of the veterans she'd seen around. She didn't recognize the other, but in the lamplight he looked quite pale. Maybe he would die, right there in the kitchen. Daddy pulled out a chair and helped lower the patient into it.

Mother took a basin from under the cupboard and handed it to the frantic Luke. "Calm down, now. Take this out on the porch and pump some water. Finas, would you stir up the fire so we can heat water and get my things from the other room?"

She drew another chair up and sat next to her patient, who wasn't nearly as upset as his friend. Maybe that was because he was about to die. Soothing the young man, Mother cut back the britches from his leg, soft voice breaking off when she saw the wound.

"However did you do this?"

Luke returned with the basin of water. "Is he okay?"

On the stove the teakettle hissed loudly, and Mother didn't answer. "Finas, could you pour some of that water into the basin? Don't get it too hot."

Though Edna was used to sick or injured people dropping by occasionally, this was the worst she'd ever seen. What if Mother couldn't do anything and he died? Right there in their kitchen. How could she be so calm? Edna sneaked farther into the room to watch Mother bathe the wound with a clean cloth. He sucked in a loud breath whenever she touched him. Water in the basin turned redder each time Mother dipped and wrung the cloth.

Backing off, Edna stumbled onto the porch, swallowing hard, and gazed at the stars to keep from puking up her guts.

Daddy always said that Mother could remove a splinter the size of a fencepost or mend scrapes and bruises better than any doctor, but this was different. At a safe distance she watched through the window while her mother handled the situation so professionally that she experienced a newfound pride. But something else became clear, as well. She definitely did not want to be a nurse. Not that she'd ever considered it seriously, but this experience certainly convinced her.

Mother was only happy when she had someone to take care of, but Edna figured she was lucky to take care of herself.

Later she learned, through her old habit of eavesdropping, that the boy's wound had gone into blood poisoning and if he hadn't gotten to Mother when he did, he probably would have died. As it was, he told everyone who would listen how Mrs. Smith had saved his life. That raised her mother up another notch in Edna's estimation.

A scant month later, she decided she wanted to be a professional cowpuncher, and announced the fact to Daddy.

He gave her the once-over in his quiet way, then smiled. "Fine with me. Going-on-fifteen is old enough to make such an important decision, I suppose. We'll let you help out with roundup."

That had been pretty easy. At a play party that weekend, she announced her plans to her friends. She also secretly told them about her idea to stay out of school the coming year. All were impressed.

"What did your folks say?" Enza Sewell asked.

"Well, I haven't exactly told them yet."

"You mean, asked them, don't you," Leonard chimed in.

Everyone laughed.

The summer flew much faster than ever before. She had to talk to Mother and Daddy soon about staying out of school for the year.

Trembling with anxiety, she waited until after supper one evening, rehearsing what she would say and how she would say it over and over while they ate.

As was their custom, they sat on the porch to watch the sun drop behind the San Juans, discussing their day. When it came her turn, she cleared her throat and made a couple of false starts.

"Well, for goodness sake, you'd think you'd been up to some troublesome deeds," Mother finally said.

"Yes, spit it out, girl, before it chokes you," Daddy joked. "I hope you haven't changed your mind about being a cowpuncher. Roundup's just around the corner."

"No, no, it's not that. I want...I wish I could...I want to stay home this winter. Not go to school." There, it was out.

They both stared at her, so before either could object, she babbled on, "I could be a big help here, you wouldn't have to hire so many hands. We'd all be together. I could make it up the next year. I only need a few extra credits to go ahead and graduate in my junior year. I'd still be out before I'm seventeen. And besides, I'm so miserable in Durango. I just want to be home with you both for a while."

She halted, held her breath and gazed at them each in turn. They appeared speechless, glancing at each other, then back at her.

Finally, both spoke at the same time.

"Well, child..." Daddy began.

"I never thought..." Mother said.

"Go ahead," Daddy said.

"You can't quit high school. You need an education."

"I don't want to quit, I just want to stay out a year. I'll go back and finish, I promise."

"Indeed you will," Daddy said.

"You mean, I can do it?" Edna's spirits soared.

"Wait a minute, I didn't mean that, not exactly." Daddy studied her fondly, then looked at Mother. "She would be a big help to me...and you too. And it would be nice to have you both here all winter. Even with the hands, I do get lonely."

"Well." Mother touched his hand, turned back to Edna. "We'll hear no excuses the following year. You will go back and finish."

"Yes, yes. I promise. Oh, thank you. Thank you." She hugged them each in turn, then ran out into the yard and whooped so loud the horses raised their heads and stared toward her.

Between parties and ranch chores, she took long rides on Tony, so relieved her happiness overflowed like the Tusas River in the spring.

Upriver near Hopewell, the Royal family had settled, and one afternoon she paid them a visit.

Approaching the Royals' ranch she could see it was well maintained. The stock looked fat and sassy, the corrals were in good shape and the house and outbuildings neatly kept.

A woman dressed in old fashioned calico came out to greet her when she rode up and dismounted.

"Hello there," she called, shading her eyes with one hand.

Edna introduced herself.

The woman's smile brightened her plain face. "I'm Eunice Royal. Why don't you come on in? Have something cool to drink. That sun's getting pretty warm."

Though Eunice was a good dozen or more years older than Edna, once the two began to talk, there was no stopping them.

Edna told about settling at Tusas and how she was staying out of school for the coming year. Eunice then told how her family had come to be in Hopewell.

"Momma's from back East, New England roots. Augusta's her name. She was teaching school and met Daddy in Kansas. He was flush at the time, struck it rich in Denver. It didn't last long, though. They came here during the mining days, and after the mines played out, we stayed. He's plenty older than her. I don't think he'll ever give up the idea of striking it rich. He wanders around all over the country side looking to hit paydirt one more time."

"Do you like to ride?" Edna asked, sipping at the cold well water Eunice had set before her.

"Oh, yes, whenever I get the chance. My brothers and I take care of the ranch, and there's some work to do, but I just take off every once in a while and leave it to Momma and the boys. Maybe we could go together sometime."

"That would be great. And maybe you could come down to Tusas. Mother loves to give parties. I'll let you know the next time and you can come."

Eunice flushed. "I'm not exactly much for parties. Reckon I've let the years pile up on me. But I'd love to ride with you sometime. Or go fishing and camping up in the mountains. That's my favorite thing to do. Just take off and stay gone a week or more. Let's the boys know just how much I do for them." Again that smile that turned her plain features pretty.

"Oh, I'd love that. Next time you want to take a trip, you let me know. I'll be ready."

"Let's plan it today," Eunice said, and joined her at the table.

When Eunice showed up the following week, Edna was surprised to see she wore a split riding skirt and boots and flop-brimmed hat. The woman didn't look much like the comely housewife she'd met at the Hopewell ranch.

Daddy watched them load their pack horse and saddle up. "Where you bound for?"

"Up on the Brazos about fifteen miles," Eunice said.

"Sounds like quite a trip. You going to fish?"

"Indeed we are."

"Well, you ladies have a good time, and bring me some of those trout."

"We'll sure do that, Mr. Smith," Eunice said.

They rode for a good portion of the day, steadily climbing. Dismounting at the river, Eunice pointed off a-ways.

"There's a cow camp cabin we can stay in. Might as well get settled before we wet a line."

Together they unpacked their gear, piled everything on the lean-to porch and unsaddled the horses. Once the animals were put out to graze, they stomped up the rickety steps.

"Look at that," Edna said, pointing to a hole gnawed in the door.

Eunice shoved the door open, and they laid out bedrolls and stored saddles and other gear inside on the dusty floor. That done, they took their poles and went to the river.

A little after dark they had caught four nice trout.

"Well, that takes care of supper," Eunice said.

They built a bonfire outside, cooked their fish and ate until they could hold no more. Both leaned back against a fallen juniper to contemplate the stars.

"Pretty, isn't it?"

"I love this country. Once I'm out of school, I'm never leaving it again," Edna replied.

"Well, I suppose not unless your folks do."

"Even then, I'd stay."

"Your dad is really a good-looking fella and your Momma's real pretty. They seem to like each other a lot."

"I guess they do." Edna was not used to discussing such personal matters, but Eunice didn't seem to hold anything sacred.

"That's nice. Momma doesn't speak to Daddy."

"Not ever?" Edna could not conceive of that.

"Well, she hasn't since he signed the boys up to go off to the war."

"Oh, my goodness. But the war's over, they must have made out okay."

"Oh, they never had to go. The war was over about two weeks after he signed them up. Still, she never forgave him. He became Mr. Royal, and she only refers to him, never speaks directly to him."

"That must be sort of hard, at times."

"Mostly, we just ignore it, me and the boys. Besides, Daddy's off most of the time trying to strike it rich again."

Edna yawned. "You think he ever will?"

"Nah."

"Well, I think it's about time to go to bed."

"Yeah."

Together they snuffed out the fire and went inside. After chatting awhile, Edna nodded off to the sound of Eunice's soft snoring.

How long she'd been asleep, she had no idea, when the biggest commotion awoke her. Eunice, too, came awake with a cry.

"What is that?" Lighting a lantern she held it high.

One of their bridles wiggled across the floor and before they could make out what was moving it, a stick of stove wood fell from the box and began to follow suit. A slab of bread took up the march.

"My goodness, what's going on?" Edna cried, pulling her feet up under her.

"Rats. Pack rats." Eunice set down the lantern and threw a stick of wood at the varmints. The furry creatures took off squealing and made it out the hole in the door.

"That ought to take care of that," Eunice said.

They put everything up out of reach and soon they had settled once more into their bedrolls.

Edna hadn't even closed her eyes good when she heard the ripping of newspapers.

Again they lit the lantern. In its dim light, a rat sat calmly on the table tearing at the newspaper that covered it. He glanced at them with beady eyes, then went back to work. Their shoes shuffled across the floor. A few of the little devils tugged at the saddles in a vain effort to steal them as well.

Eunice laughed. "Whoa, now. You'll never get those through that itty bitty hole."

Shooing the rat off the table, Edna tiptoed gingerly through the clutter of belongings. "Let's plug it up, maybe that'll help."

By then both were laughing hysterically at the antics of the pack rats.

Heaving her saddle onto a high shelf, and picking up Edna's, Eunice asked, "What do you suppose they were going to do with these if they got them out the door? Go riding?"

"Wouldn't surprise me. We'd better tuck everything away good before we plug up that hole. Just in case."

Once that was accomplished, they nestled down into their beds.

"I can just see Tony trotting along with a pack rat on his back," Edna said, and broke into giggles.

"I wonder if my shoes would've fit the one who was stealing them?" Eunice said between giggles.

It was a long time before they could stop laughing and settle down. Obviously they had discouraged the rats, because they slept the remainder of the night with no more interruptions.

In spite of the differences in their ages, Edna enjoyed the outing with Eunice more than anything she had ever done.

The remainder of the summer the two rode many long happy hours together. Often they would scout out the stray cattle as they'd wandered afar and could tell the hands where they were come roundup time.

Eager to take part in the roundup, Edna mentioned it to her father one evening when the nights had begun to grow frosty and the wind carried a bite to it.

He glanced at Mother, then nodded.

"I'll wake you up in the morning. Be ready to go."

It seemed she had hardly put her head on the pillow and closed her eyes when he shook her awake.

"Get up sleepy head, time's a wasting. Get dressed and get yourself a sandwich. We have to go find some strays."

"What time is it?"

"Mmm. I don't know. About five, I reckon. Maybe earlier."

Head in her hands, she sat on the edge of the bed. Daddy hadn't said anything about waking up in the middle of the night. Was this really what she wanted?

"Get a move on," Daddy shouted.

Grumbling to herself she quickly dressed in britches and flannel shirt, stuffed her feet into thick socks and riding boots and stumbled into the kitchen.

Mother had their lunches packed and after a quick breakfast they took off. The general principle of the roundup at Tusas was to find all the cattle hiding in gullies or halfway up the mountain side or off somewhere on forestry land, then bring them in to the corrals. There they would be tallied, culled and the calves branded. Then they would be driven to lower range for the winter.

Dawn of that first day found her working her way up a draw thick with prickly, low-growing pinon that reached long branches out to grab at her pant legs. Tony picked his way through sagebrush and chamisa without balking, but search as she might she couldn't find one single head. Disheartened, she rejoined Daddy and they broke for lunch, sitting under a tree to eat their sandwich and sip water from a canteen. In less than thirty minutes they were back in the saddle again. They rode and searched out cattle hard as they could till almost dark. Driving some twenty head, they finally started back to the ranch.

"Well, how did it go?" Mother asked while they ate a cold supper.

"Fine. She's doing great, Mother. I think we've got ourselves a professional cowgirl here. I do believe in another year or so I can let go a couple of the hands and she can take their place."

Edna picked at her food in silence. Riding the valley was one thing, but this…not what she'd expected at all. Maybe tomorrow would be better.

After supper she fell into bed with a groan.

The next morning when Daddy shook her awake it was raining. What a miserable day. Still, she persevered. Hunched under heavy rubber rain gear, water dripping off the brim of her hat and running down the back of her neck, she trailed one bone headed steer after another. Inside thick leather gloves her fingers were numb and cold.

"Might as well skip lunch and get this done," Daddy said when she herded a cow and calf to him.

Despite an empty hole in her stomach, she agreed. Maybe he'd quit early. But he didn't. It was nearing dark when they put the thirty or so soaked, stinking cattle in the corral and made their muddy way to the house.

Two or three times during supper, she tried to tell Daddy she'd changed her mind about being a cowpuncher, but couldn't get the words out of her mouth. He'd be so disappointed in her. Besides, Mother and Daddy kept looking at each other with those knowing smirks. They expected her to quit. And oh, how she wanted to, but she ate hurriedly and crawled into bed, determined to see this done.

She made it one more day. Out of bed in the pitch black, riding all day in search of some lunk-headed cows too stupid to find their way home; wading mud and dragging a bellering calf from the river; returning home tired and sore to the bone.

On the fourth day, when Daddy shook her, she refused to get out of bed.

After a while, he went away, and she heard him announce in a loud voice that he figured Edna's cowgirl days were over. She also heard the general laughter from all the hands and Mother too, but sleep overtook her before she could care.

It wasn't until many years later that she thought about that roundup. He never ran roundups like that before. Instead, he and some hands would ride out about eight o'clock and return home around four or five. Then maybe he wouldn't go out again for several days. It sometimes took a couple of weeks for them to gather the herd and ready it for winter pasture. He had been teaching her a lesson.

The joke was on her and, at the time she hadn't even seen it.

Chapter Eleven

Edna's Diary—1929

I so look forward to spending this year here on the ranch. Wish I never had to go back to school. But I'm not going to think about that.

Funny, everyone thinks Leonard and I are going steady. That's because he's such a dreamy dancer that I make sure he's on my program a lot. We never think of it as going steady. He's in love with a woman in Texas, but the family is against them marrying because she's a divorcee with two kids and he's just out of high school. I have no thoughts about marrying anyone.

Early that spring while snow still nestled in the hollows and on the northern slopes and the distant mountains glistened in the sunlight, a visitor showed up at the ranch.

Dad greeted the fellow in the yard, and Edna hung around close enough to hear what was going on.

"Name's Quesenberry," the lanky young man said. "I'm the extension agent from down at the college in Las Cruces. And it's our idea to talk a few of you ranchers into raising high altitude potatoes. Up in the San Luis Valley they're getting ready to plant most of their fields in Red McClures."

Daddy scratched his head and stared out across his land. "I don't know. Times are tough enough without trying something new we aren't sure will work."

"Oh, it'll work all right," Quesenberry said. "It's just a matter of getting them in the ground soon. We'll supply the first year's seed

potatoes and fertilizer. You get the ground plowed up and ready. I'm
going to talk to your neighbor, Mr. McCowan, and some others.
Appreciate if you could get on board with this. We believe you can
make a good crop and there'll be some money in it too. These days,
that's nothing to scoff at."

When Quesenberry left, Daddy talked to Mother a while about
the possibilities.

"What are the boys going to think of changing over from being
cowpunchers to farmers?" she asked.

"Since they're all pretty glad to have a paying job, I figure they'll
do whatever is offered. Besides, I don't intend to give up raising
stock. Reckon they can have their pick. I'll talk to some of the other
fellows about it first, see what they think, but that young fella pretty
well sold me on it."

And so that spring they plowed up the pastures and planted
potatoes, like the owners of all the little ranches around them. The
Great Depression held them in its grip and, along with the sheep and
cattle, raising a food crop was a living.

Finas had bought forty or so old ewes and bred them. Because
Edna was home, it became her job to keep the flock inside the fence.
What a treasure those days were. With book in hand, she would set
out. The only problem was she'd often become so absorbed in
reading that she'd look up and discover the sheep had gone astray.
Even though that meant crawling through the fence and wandering
the hills in search of them, she liked the job much better than
handling cattle. In fact, she became rather fond of some of the old
ladies and gave them names to suit their personalities.

The ewes dutifully produced lambs, and instead of selling them,
Daddy kept them.

"We'll soon have a nice herd," he told her. "Good idea to have
some sheep to support the ups and downs of cattle prices. Wool holds
more or less a steady price. Besides, they're easier handled. And we
have to wait and see about the potatoes."

She worried what he'd do when she went back to school, but that
wasn't a thing she wanted to think about or bring up.

Later that spring a letter arrived from Kentucky. Finas handed it to Cassie without comment, though he appeared uneasy.

She read the letter from his mother, then folded it carefully and lay it on the table. "I don't know what else to do, Finas, but have them come here."

The anxiety cleared from his expression. "I just wanted to make sure it's all right with you. Looks like Mom and Dad are having a really hard time of it back in Kentucky. If they come live here, it'll be easier than us trying to do something for them from this distance."

She nodded, mind already on restructuring the rooms to accommodate the elder Smiths.

"Okay, then, I'll write and let them know, then arrange passes on the train."

"Will you be going to get them?"

"I don't think so. They're not exactly infirm. Besides, I'll need to stay here and supervise building them a place to live. Probably best if we just add on a room big enough for them to be independent."

"I could go get them," she offered.

He put an arm around her. "They'll be fine. Someone's got to cook for the hands."

Disappointed, Cassie didn't tell Finas that she would have welcomed taking the train to Kentucky and back. The winter had been long and harsh, and the trip would be fun. But he was right. Edna couldn't handle the cooking for everyone all alone, it took the two of them to feed such a crew three meals a day.

Edna enjoyed living at home and helping out with chores both in the house and on the ranch. Like any girl her age she also liked to go to parties and dance, and so looked forward to snow melt when they could once more travel. She would be fifteen that July, but her parents refused to allow her to go to dances without a chaperone. That didn't mean she couldn't go, and it certainly didn't mean she couldn't hook up with her favorite partners, once there. She had been asked to be one of the accompanists on the piano at church sings, and that was a treat as well.

After grumbling her way through piano lessons in North Dakota, she was surprised to so enjoy playing for fun and sharing music brought her and Mother closer as well.

Often that summer she and Mother talked Daddy into taking them to a dance at the school house in Tres Piedras. Though he acted like he minded, Daddy really enjoyed gathering with the other ranchers to talk about crops and prices and this new potato venture. As for Mother, she welcomed visiting with the women from surrounding ranches. Florida McCowan would be there, and since the Naylors had moved away, she and Florida had become closer.

"I feel sorry for that boy of hers," Mother would say. "It's like she doesn't even know he exists once he's out of bed and fed breakfast. All Florida knows how to do is work and make money. I swear, I never saw a woman who could outwork her."

Privately, Edna wondered why anyone would even try. She loved Florida dearly, but wondered why she considered money more important than anything else. If you asked her where she got a dress, her reply would be how much it cost. Ask if she sold out the last order of feed, she'd quote how much she made off the sale.

"She thinks she's going to die young, like the rest of her family," Cassie explained. "And she wants to put back enough money to care for the boy." Cassie shook her head. "Too bad she doesn't see he'd rather have her looking after him now. Besides, she'll probably outlive us all."

Daddy took them to the dance. The boy from Servilleta, her first true boyfriend, with whom she'd danced since she was twelve, had moved away, but there were plenty of others. So many, in fact, that she and the other girls made out a program to make sure they danced with each one.

She spent the first hour or so dodging Albert Hanaway. Each time he headed toward her, she found another boy eager to dance. Albert was tall, lanky and awkward. His hands were soft and squishy, and he greased his hair down till it gleamed.

Lots of Mexican families came to the dance, but they usually didn't mix with the Anglos. However, this night, one of the older Mexican boys strode boldly across the floor to claim her hand before the next boy on her program could approach.

133

Her heart bounced around in her chest, and she looked around for help.

Someone touched her shoulder. "Hey, kid. Ain't this my dance?"

She turned and saw Albert. Her heart dropped into her stomach. No choice, she dare not dance with the Mexican boy, and Daddy, who usually rescued her on such an occasion, was in a far corner deep in conversation with several ranchers.

The Mexican boy hesitated a moment, holding on to her, making her heart jitter. Fights sometimes broke out, but she had never been the object of one. The boy looked at Albert, back at her, then shrugged and moved away.

She slipped into Albert's arms as they swung into a waltz. "Thank you," she whispered, ashamed that she had avoided him earlier.

"It's okay. My dad told me how everyone used to come to the dances armed. He said never a Saturday night went by someone didn't get shot or shot at for just such as that. No Mexican should dance with an Anglo girl. I was afraid he might have a gun."

"I hope you weren't going to shoot him." She giggled nervously.

Albert chuckled, stumbled and caught the rhythm again. "Nah, I don't even own a gun."

When the music stopped, she pulled out her program. "Thanks. Leonard has the next dance."

"You're welcome," Albert murmured.

After that, she made sure to always include Albert in her program for at least one dance, even though he wasn't the best dancer and the stuff he plastered his hair down with smelled sweet as a woman's perfume.

With Grandpa and Grandma Smith on the ranch, there was more to do than ever. They pretty much took care of themselves, but they did expect a certain amount of attention, especially from their granddaughter. Grandma was a sweet little woman who never raised her voice, nor had a bad thing to say about anyone. Edna might get her tiny size from Grandma, but she guessed it wasn't in the cards for her to be more like her. Speaking her mind seemed ingrained so deeply she couldn't help it, even when she knew there might be trouble because of it.

Grandpa had a lovely great mustache. He was smaller and quieter than Daddy, and liked to take long walks and that became worrisome sometimes. Being so quiet, he could be gone a long time before anyone missed him.

"Where's Grandpa?" Mother would ask.

Edna knew what that meant. Go find your grandpa, that's what. Sometimes, she felt closer to Gram and Gramps than her own parents because she had lived with them from three to six years old.

And so the summer of 1929 passed. The time for returning to school came and went without mention, and Edna's happiness at remaining at home for the coming winter grew.

November, and the evenings had grown chill; by morning frosts laced the sage like jewels.

Still Cassie enjoyed sitting on the porch next to Finas to watch darkness creep across the desert from the distant mountains. This particular evening, he joked about the upcoming Thanksgiving gathering at Rome and Mamie Sewell's.

"Reckon I ought to try to round up a turkey?"

She smacked playfully at him. "Will I never live that down? Mae and I were laughing about it in Durango." She paused, clasped his hand. "I wish she could be with us."

"I know, but I'm glad you'll be here this year."

"I just hope Edna doesn't give us a hard time when we send her back to school next year. But she's still so young, I don't think it's hurt her a bit being out for a year, especially the way she feels about going."

"Is it Durango she hates, or just the idea of being away from home?"

"She doesn't like the school there much, but being anywhere but here isn't going to make her happy. That's the reason she's going to take extra courses and get out early. After missing a year she still won't even be seventeen when she graduates."

"I'm not sure I understand her connection to the ranch. She doesn't like most of the work involved. Put her to work picking up potatoes this fall and she loafed around, missing half and falling behind all the others."

"Oh, so true." Cassie laughed. "And the time she wanted to be a cowpuncher."

It was Finas' turn to laugh. "Well, I think it's her age, that's all. She's young and still wants to have fun. She'll settle down to something soon. She managed to get meals on the table for six hands after she traded potato picking jobs with you."

"Yes, she did that, but if it hadn't been for Mom she never would've."

"Well, then, see?"

"Oh, Finas. You'd take her side no matter what she did."

He laughed. "I reckon I probably would. She's such a sweetheart."

"She is that."

"Why don't we see if there isn't someplace else she can go to finish school? It could make a great deal of difference."

She nodded. "What a good idea. I'll write to Mae and see if she has any suggestions. Maybe we can come up with something."

"Good. I hate to see our girl unhappy."

"Me too. Yet, I'm afraid she'll never be happy anywhere but at Tusas. I so want her to go to college, but she seems so indifferent."

The last of the sun's dying rays painted a blaze of orange and gold over the San Juan's.

He smiled and rubbed her hand. "Don't worry about our Edna. She's smart enough to realize she will have to do something soon. One thing's for sure, we can't force her to go to college. We'll just give her some time."

"We'll see. I don't suppose we can make her do anything, headstrong as she is. My folks tried to make me do things I didn't want to do, and later it was so difficult to go my own way. I felt like I couldn't be trusted to make my own decisions."

In silence, they watched the sky darken and the first stars shimmer to life in the ashen sky. "Isn't it beautiful?" she murmured, still holding his warm hand.

"Mmm. I remember a time when you couldn't bear the thought of staying here."

"Yes, well, it's still sometimes not easy. And I do appreciate getting away now and then to practice nursing. I'll go with Edna next year. Wherever we send her, I'm sure I can get a nursing job." She held her breath waiting for his reply. One day would he balk at her desire to spread her wings occasionally?

In the dark, his lips touched the tips of her fingers. "I know. It's hard on you being out here."

The tone of his voice let her know he might understand, but he sure didn't like it. That was what a good marriage was about, though, wasn't it? Putting the partner's feelings first when it really mattered.

"Now, what's going on at the Sewells' house?"

"Well, there'll be Rome's family and Mamie's brother Leonard Gipson, Ford Bradley, the May family, the Patchens, and McCrakens and Wootens and us. I think that's all. And of course all the youngsters, about ten I think, if we counted right."

When she shivered, he put an arm around her shoulder. "Getting cold, let's go inside."

She followed him through the door as they continued to chat about the gathering that would signal the end of such get-togethers for the winter. No one went much of anywhere except by sled once the snows fell. That's when she was the most lonely. But the boys who helped work the ranch had become more like family, so it wasn't too bad.

The settling of this country was in the hands of the very people she knew so well. Some would probably be remembered and written up in history books. And of course, there were their acquaintances in Taos. The artists who were already famous and some who would be one day: Allen McFee, Burt Phillips, Helen Blumenschein, Kenneth Adams, and Blanche Chloe Grant. She appreciated getting to know all the important families. It satisfied the Cooney in her.

Edna could hardly wait until Thanksgiving. She and Leonard got along well. Her cousin, Marvin Baker, had come out to work for Dad this past summer and had stayed on. He and Enza Sewell were chummy, though he complained that she bored him.

She remembered the first time the four of them had gotten together.

Mother had fed about twenty people that particular Sunday, and the younger ones would have to wash the dishes.

"Let's play croquet. Couple that loses has to wash the dishes," Enza suggested.

Edna wasn't wild about washing the dishes, and figured if she teamed up with Leonard, who was a better player, they had a chance of winning.

The two girls had to shame the boys into the challenge.

"Yeah, you figured us girls would do the dishes and you'd get out of it," she told them.

"I can wash dishes if I absolutely have to," Marvin bragged. "But this sounds like a good idea. Me and Enza can beat the two of you. Easy."

So the game was on.

After several frenzied rounds, with Marvin and Enza ahead, Edna tapped the ball on the final stroke and watched it bump the hoop and skew to one side.

Marvin hooted, grabbed Enza and whirled her around. "Good game, kid," he said.

Enza laughed. "We had to win, I hate doing dishes. Did you see that mess in the kitchen?"

"Sure did. Wouldn't want to have to wash all them."

"Darn," Leonard said in his good-natured way. "I can't believe we lost."

Edna shrugged. "Could be worse."

"Oh, yeah? How's that?" He joined Marvin in gathering up the hoops, balls and mallets and stowing them.

"Swamping out horse stalls, for one. Or pulling a calf. Or horsing a bone-headed cow out of a mud hole. Ugh."

Leonard took her hand and swung it playfully. "You're right, I'm grateful. In fact, I'll wash and you can dry. You know where they all go."

Marvin stared at him in disbelief. "You really going to help her? Boys don't wash dishes. You and me can ride over to Tusas and get some pop. These girls will be thirsty when they finish."

"Wait a minute," Enza said. "We won."

"Yea, but everyone knows washing dishes is for girls." Marvin tossed her a wicked grin, and both girls yelped and chased him around and around before giving up catching him.

"I'm staying here...helping Edna," Leonard said. "That was the deal we made."

"I can't believe you're serious," Marvin said.

The two of them sat on the porch and hooted at Edna and Leonard while they cleaned up the kitchen.

Grateful to Leonard for standing up against Marvin's teasing, she looked forward to seeing him again at the Thanksgiving gathering.

There would be six more kids around their age. The river had frozen over last week, and so they planned to ice skate. The ten of them would share two pair of skates, so it would be two at a time and she and Leonard would make a good couple. Those waiting their turn could always get up a game of encino or penny poker. Or maybe spin the bottle. It promised to be a fun day. Especially since she didn't have to think about returning to Durango the following week.

For Mom, winters were boring on the ranch, but Edna enjoyed them. Gramps insisted on saddling Tony for her, after which she would mount up and ride off into the cold. The crunch of hooves in the snow, the silence broken only by the wind high in the trees, her breath rising in clouds. All the best. The very best.

Some days she rode to the post office in Tusas, others she walked the mile and a half, bundled against the cold. Stomping off her boots, she'd head inside where the pot-bellied stove poured heat into the store. How fun to joke with Mr. Gallegos and anyone else gathered there. Sometimes she'd pick up something for Mom for supper.

The wonderful days of freedom stretched out before her. This was the life she wanted. Always.

The summer of 1930 flashed by so quickly she could barely hang onto the days. She would be sixteen in July, and then in late August she would have to return to school. Though she pushed the thought aside, it remained there. A threat she couldn't deny, no matter how hard she tried.

What with Saturday night dances and parties at the ranch, she managed to put off any discussion of returning to school until Mother and Daddy brought it up one evening just before her birthday party. Supper was over, the kitchen cleaned, and the family on the front porch. She could hear the hands playing poker around the other side of the bunkhouse and wished they'd invited her to join them.

Then Mother said something to her that doubled and tripled that wish.

"I've been in touch with Mae, and she's looked into your going to high school in Salida this fall. We thought you might like it better than Durango."

For a long while, Edna stared off into the distance, the evening sky all lavenders and purples chased by the approaching darkness. She took a big breath.

"Don't sigh at me, young lady," Mother said sternly.

"I wasn't sighing. Really."

"Umm, well. It's not too soon to talk about it. Your father and I thought you might like the change. I'll have to get your records transferred over there, and we can take you up a week or so early so you can arrange for those extra courses you wanted to take to finish this year."

Couldn't Mother have waited until after her party this weekend before bringing this up? Now that would be all she could think about.

"Edna, answer your Mother," Daddy said.

"What? Yes, fine."

"Just think, darling," Mother said in her soothing tone. "Only one year and you'll graduate. Since you'll not be seventeen yet, there'll be no hurry about getting on with your life.

There, now she had to go and bring that up. Bad enough to have to think of going back to school, but to have to figure out getting on with her life when she was having so much fun here on the ranch. Well, that was too much.

Edna followed Mother off the train in Salida and left behind her childhood. Where had the time gone?

High school in Salida turned out to be much the same as Durango. Perhaps it wasn't the place, but her reluctance to leave her beloved childhood behind that made her so miserable.

Oh, school was okay, she supposed. She made some friends and went to dances and studied hard so she would never have to come back again. She would never have to be sixteen again and do what everyone else told her. One day, she would run her own life, do as she pleased. But that day was sure a long time in coming.

Finally, it was time to graduate and go home.

At long last it was over. And Mother and Daddy wanted her to stay home till she was eighteen before going off to college. They didn't have to ask twice. Nothing much had changed at Tusas—not that she'd wanted it to—and she fell back into the ranch routine as if she'd never been away.

Daddy had hired Mexican sheep herders for his growing herd. He figured in another year or so he'd have about 200 head.

That summer Uncle Perk and Aunt Bonnie and their three-year-old son Marshall, came to live. By that time Daddy had bought the place above Tusas and the Perkins moved into the log cabin up there. Aunt Bonnie was Dad's sister. They had gone to Detroit, along with a lot of other Kentucky families, to work in the car plants before the Great Depression. When there was no more work, they had to do something.

Eavesdropping, she learned that Grams had talked Daddy into asking them to come to the ranch. Often she overheard things that made her wonder at the complexity of life.

One of their Mexican sheep herders once said to Daddy, "You know, there are three peoples here in this area. My people, your people and the Texans."

Another time Mother told Daddy: "Your mother thinks we're rich."

He laughed. "I guess so."

"She does. Marvin told me that when she heard he was out of work she wrote him and told him to come out here. Said Finas has that big ranch, he'll put you to work. Marvin said she was always writing letters back east telling how rich we are. That's probably why Bonnie and Perk came."

"Reckon they'll all find out different soon enough."

Mother was quiet for a while. "I don't know. We do have this big ranch, we raise all those potatoes. We never go hungry and we do have nice things. Maybe we are rich, Finas."

"Compared to some, I suppose."

"From what I hear, compared to many. There are places where folks are starving, standing in bread lines."

"Well," Daddy said, "if the hard work don't kill us, I expect we won't starve." He took Mother's hand and patted it. "There are some ways in which we're very rich."

Mother remained still, but Edna could imagine her flushing at the compliment.

Studying her father, she decided hard work was good for him. He had survived a disease that killed many, and though he wasn't strong enough to run the ranch alone, he certainly did his share of work.

How many times she wished she were a man and could take over for him. Clearly she wasn't big enough to do it, but one day she hoped to at least help in the running of the place.

One Sunday, soon after Aunt Bonnie and Uncle Perk arrived, they were at the house for dinner. Edna casually listened to the talk going around the table.

"Did you get settled?" Mother asked.

Aunt Bonnie smiled, her eyes sparkling. "Yes, the place is small, but good for us. I'm glad we came, it's beautiful out here. But what do you do for fun?"

Daddy laughed heartily. "You mean you aren't having any fun?"

Mother joined in. "Goodness, I'd have thought brushing away all those spider webs and mud swallow's nests would've been a joy."

Edna could hold her tongue no longer. "We go to dances on Saturday nights in Tres Piedras…that is when we can get Daddy to take us. I'm too young to go without a chaperone." She aimed a stern gaze her father's way, and he chuckled.

"Child would rather dance than eat or sleep."

Aunt Bonnie clapped her hands with glee. "Oh, Perk and I love to dance. He's a dancing fool, aren't you?"

The taciturn man smiled. "Wouldn't do me not to be. That woman wears out shoes dancing."

Edna could scarcely contain herself. "Then you could be my chaperone...couldn't you?"

Everyone looked at everyone else around the table. Adults had a terrible way of communicating without saying a word. A raised eyebrow, a down-turned mouth, a shake of the head spoke tons.

"Then we could go every Saturday, not just once in a while, couldn't we?"

Daddy shook his head, and she readied herself for an argument, then he nodded. "I'd welcome someone taking over my chore. I enjoy going once a month or so, but every Saturday's just more than I can bear."

"Then it's settled," Edna said, jumping up so quickly she jarred the table. Daddy was right. She'd rather dance than eat.

And so 1931 passed in a blur of dancing and parties and ranch chores and long winter months that were no longer lonely with so many people living at Tusas.

She would turn eighteen in July 1932, and still had no idea of what she wanted to do. It was like some kind of deadline loomed over her, pushing her to let go everything that brought enjoyment.

And then the best thing that could've happened did. Mother received a letter from the Naylors saying that Nell Frances was recovering from pneumonia and could she spend her recovery at Tusas. Life could not have been better. Her friend arrived in time for Edna's birthday party.

"Isn't 1932 a great time to be eighteen?" Edna asked her friend, who laughed.

"I guess so, I just wish I were."

"Oh, that's right, you're still a baby. Just wait till next year. Wherever we are, we'll have to get together to celebrate your becoming an adult. And then 1933 will be a great year to be eighteen."

"Hey," Nell hollered, then they grabbed onto each other and rocked back and forth, laughing.

Nell had lost some weight and was still pale, but she recovered quickly in the healthy high desert air and sunshine. She was soon well enough to enjoy all the activities.

Every Saturday or Sunday, depending on what else was going on, the Tres Piedras baseball team played one of its rivals.

The whole community would load into a couple of two-ton trucks and take off for Taos Junction, Taos or Antonito. The fellows pitched in what they could to buy gas. Twenty cents a gallon meant a lot of money. At least once each trip one of the old trucks would break down. Repairs were done by whoever was clever enough with bailing wire and chewing gum.

Tres Piedras had a star pitcher by the name of Leon Carpenter, who drove his own little Ford.

The day they soundly beat Taos 16-2 was to become legendary. It wasn't the game so much as what happened afterward that lent to the legend.

Edna and Nell rode in the back of one of the old trucks, and as they left the baseball field, Leon led the parade into the Taos square. It was a quiet night, with a few people strolling or sitting on benches in the center of the square. As Leon made it halfway around, he stuck his head out the window and began to shout. Over and over as he circled, he yelled whoopee at the top of his lungs.

Everyone thought they might follow suit, but hesitated when the town constable pulled Leon's little Ford over. Afraid of what might happen, the rest of the crowd hustled out of town as quiet as could be.

Next day they found out that Leon had spent the night in jail because he disturbed the peace.

"Reckon the town fathers couldn't stand so much glee," he explained to everyone after he hustled home to Tres Piedras the next day.

There was a dance hall built of slabs up in the woods. There dances were held every two weeks. They would all load into Uncle

Perk's '28 Chevy and go sailing down the road, singing all the way, "Let Me Call You Sweetheart," "Wedding Bells," "It's a Long Way to Tipperary," "Red River," and any other songs Aunt Bonnie knew the words to. The off weeks were dances in Taos Junction. They also had a slab hall built by their American Legion ex-World War One fellows.

One night Nell and Edna decided to give the crowd a treat. They wore their high school prom dresses. Edna's was turquoise crepe de chine and Nell's was pink. They walked in the door and Leon greeted them with, "Why, hell, the kids are all growed up."

And Edna was surprised to realize that she did indeed feel "all growed up." And it wasn't near as bad as she'd imagined.

Very often the dances broke up because of a fight. There were even guns displayed. No one was ever seriously hurt.

There were play parties at Katie Ford's, at the Gentrys, the Sewells and at Edna's house. These were just that. They would spend an evening playing silly games and having contests. Or playing croquet or tennis. No expensive equipment, just the basic flat space and simple tools. Serious competition eliminated teams until the final losers had to wash the dishes or push the winners in a wheelbarrow.

That final summer of their youth, Nell and Edna rode horse back all over the hills and walked for miles. They fished. They helped with chores. They talked themselves hoarse. They had a glorious time.

It was a fitting goodbye to their carefree childhood, and they did it up right.

Chapter Twelve

Edna's Diary—1932

The funniest thing. Mother and Daddy went with us to a dance over at Tres Piedras earlier this summer and someone referred to Daddy as Old Man Smith. This is the way people refer to most middle-aged adults around here, but no one had ever done it with my folks till now. When we got home, Mother threw a wall-eyed fit, said they weren't going to become Old Man and Old Lady Smith, just 'cause their daughter was now grown. It seems she had told them so in no uncertain terms. Wish I could've heard that, but I was on the dance floor.

Right there in front of everyone she called Daddy Pop. From that time on he's been Pop Smith to everyone and Mother is Mom, and today I called him Pop for the first time. It just slipped out because of hearing it so much of late. His eyes got wide, but I could tell he was pleased, even thought it funny.

Besides running the ranch, Pop still works as relief operator, sometimes dispatcher for the Chili Line. He's been doing so since 1925, and the little narrow gauge train remains busy as can be. Freight trains, oil trains, cattle trains and passenger trains run every day from Alamosa to Durango stopping at all the little stations in between.

Over the years Mom has nursed in Santa Fe, Roswell, Alamosa, Durango and Salida. Seeing how hard they work gets me to thinking that maybe it's time I earned my own way.

Reading over that latest diary entry didn't help Edna decide how she planned to earn her own way.

Mom got into the act as well, declaring one morning, "It's time to do something with your life."

And she was right. But what?

"I think I have to stop lolling around on the ranch having a good time with no thoughts of a future," she said, and turned to face her friend Nell.

"So, what exactly are you going to do?" Nell plumped her pillow and dropped onto the bed.

"Mom wrote Uncle Bob, her brother." Edna rolled back the covers and crawled in beside her friend. "He and Aunt Margaret live in California."

"California, gee whiz."

"Yeah."

"Well, that's exciting."

"Yeah, I guess."

"Hmmm, it is kinda scary. What'll you do out there?"

"Probably stay with them and go to junior college." She rolled her eyes. "I have to babysit the two kids and help Aunt Margaret out in return."

"Sounds like a mother plan, all right."

"To tell the truth, it is." Edna rolled her eyes again. "Also sounds like I'd better agree to it."

"Wow. I envy you. I have to go back home and finish high school."

"Ugh."

Long after Nell fell asleep, Edna lay awake staring out the window at the velvety sky ablaze with trillions of stars. If only she could reach out and grab on to one. Just hang on and float away. Tears filled her eyes. Why did things have to change? She'd wanted to be eighteen and make her own decisions, like it might be some magic age. But so far, everyone else was telling her what to do, looking at her like "When are you going to act your age?" Growing up was the pits, the very pits, especially when it meant leaving Tusas.

The remainder of Mom's plans came clear the next day when she announced that the Quesenberries would pick up the two girls the following week and take them to Las Cruces for a couple of days.

Nell and Edna exchanged glances.

"And Nell's parents will come get you there. You can go to Arizona with Nell and spend a week. Then you'll board the train for Ventura." Mom beamed as if she had successfully arranged a party for seven hundred people.

Though she looked forward to such a fine trip, school loomed in Edna's future like a desert dust storm, angry and gritty.

"I'll hate it, I know I will," she told Nell.

"Well, of course you will. You absolutely must hate it. Think of all the boys…and the parties…and the dances. I've heard stories that would curl your hair."

"Mine's already curly," Edna said, refusing to allow Nell to lighten her mood.

A week at the Naylors' house flew by and way too soon, Edna boarded a train bound for California, waving through the glass at Nell and her parents. Summer was over, childhood behind her. It was time to be a big girl, to grow up and take her medicine.

She majored in home ec, because she could think of nothing else, and that would come in handy when she married. Though who she might marry totally escaped her.

None of the old bachelors would do. Offhand she couldn't think of anyone she would want to marry. Certainly not the McCowans' nephew, Calvin Hiller. He couldn't even dance. All he could do was toss people out of his aunt and uncle's dance hall. Besides, they fought about everything. Everything that is but music. They both loved swing, but you sure couldn't get serious over someone because of that one thing, could you?

Home ec would have to do even if she didn't have any prospects. She hated chemistry and stuff like that, so why not?

College turned out to be the next thing to being in hell. California was so…so crowded and noisy, and there was no winter, not like she was used to.

Margaret Ann and Bill Bob, the two Cooney cousins she babysat for the privilege of living in California with Uncle Bob and Aunt Margaret, were noisy, impossibly childish little demons. Sometimes she herself acted worse than they did. Poor Aunt Margaret.

And then something wonderful happened. After six months of dramatic suffering, she found herself enjoying school. She made some friends, met some boys who could actually dance and mended her relationship with Uncle Bob and Aunt Margaret and the kids.

The last four months were enjoyable, and then it was time to go home for the summer. It seemed she was always leaving something she loved just as she learned to love it. There might be a lesson there somewhere.

Bidding goodbye to all her friends and her aunt and uncle and cousins, she boarded the train. Pop had sent train fare and pullman money and she had ten dollars to spend on meals. Mom and Florida would meet her in Albuquerque.

In Gallup she bought the last meal she would eat on the train and had a quarter left. Now, what to do? She would need to tip the porter, but what if no one was at the station to meet her and she needed the money to make a phone call? For those last, endless miles, she worried over that quarter. But she needn't have. Even before the train hissed and screeched to a halt at the depot, she spotted Florida McCowan, who always managed to stand out in a crowd.

The porter got his quarter tip. And she was home once again, home to ride over the ranch on her favorite horse, and go to dances every Saturday night, filling her program to overflowing. The boys weren't like the college guys in Ventura. And of course, there was Calvin to fuss with. She had a wonderful summer.

When it came time to go back to school in the fall, she left with an entirely different attitude. This time, not to California. She vowed things would be better from the start of this newest adventure.

Nell and her mother had moved to Albuquerque so she could attend school, and so Edna enrolled at the university there as well, and lived with them. Nell's dad, who was still a forest ranger, was soon transferred to Albuquerque and joined them.

Having fun in college was more fun than studying. And when she was asked to pledge a sorority, she excitedly called Pop and asked him to sell Tony so she could become a sorority sister.

He was quiet on the other end of the line for a long spell. Then, "Are you sure about this, Edna?"

"Yes, Pop. Absolutely. On campus you're no one if you're not pledged." In her secret heart of hearts she hoped Pop would send her the money and she wouldn't have to sell her beloved horse, but he didn't make the offer. She was, after all, a grown-up.

"Okay, sweetheart. If you're sure. I won't have any trouble selling him. Are you learning anything down there?"

She didn't want to tell him what she was really learning, so just replied, "Sure, Pop. Plenty. Will you wire me the money as soon as you can?"

"Okay. You take care of yourself."

"I will. Thanks, Pop."

"Uh-huh," he said and disconnected.

After the Thanksgiving holidays, which Edna spent with the Naylors, she went back to school determined to study harder. She'd flunked chemistry and been called on the carpet by the actives. Still, she couldn't figure out why she needed to know anything about chemistry. Keeping house and throwing parties for a handsome husband, whom she still hadn't met, didn't call for chemical formulas.

She should have known better than to believe things could go along smoothly for long, she really should have. A few months later, when a letter came from Mom and Pop, she ripped it open while humming "Let Me Call You Sweetheart." Her monthly $10 check was due and the money for her room and board with the Naylors.

But there were no checks, only a short letter.

> *Dearest Edna,*
> *Your dad and I have to ask you to leave school*
> *and come home. A job of teaching at Taos Junction*
> *has opened, and since it is difficult for us to come up*

> *with your room and board money and expenses, we*
> *thought it best if you take the job. That way you can*
> *make your own money. After all, you'll soon be*
> *twenty and all grown up.*
>
>   *Enclosed is your pass to come home on the train.*
> *Let us know when you'll be here and we'll pick you*
> *up at the station.*
>   *All our love,*
>   *Mother and Daddy*

And so she ripped herself out by the roots once more, like some flower always being transplanted, bid goodbye to her friends and returned to Tusas.

It was no surprise to anyone when she got the teaching job at Taos Junction. After all, she had almost two years of college. Not many educated teachers were willing to sit in a one-room log schoolhouse teaching a dozen children for $53 a month.

They called her Miss Edna. Miss Smith would never have done, since they all knew her as Edna. The school room had real desks and a blackboard. Out of her check she paid room and board of $25 to the Patchen family, who ran a boarding house in town. The rest was hers to spend any way she wished.

Four of the children were from the Brazel family. Their mother strongly believed in their good behavior and respect. On April Fool's Day, which fell on a Friday, the Brazels ran off to the woods and stayed all afternoon. When the bus came they hurried in and boarded. Monday morning they marched into the school room like little angels. Miss Edna didn't say a word until recess time. Then she stood before the class and announced, "The Brazel children will have no recess until they make up the three hours they played in the woods Friday."

They took their punishment pretty well for a couple of days. Wednesday, when recess time came around, she looked up from her desk to see four wide-eyed children standing around her desk.

"Miss Edna, please let us go out and play," the oldest said.

The youngest held her hands under her chin as if praying. "Please, please."

The others echoed and gazed at her so forlornly that she gave in. "I hope you've learned your lesson."

Four heads nodded vigorously. "Yes, Miss Edna. Oh, yes, we have."

And indeed, it appeared they had.

And so, once again, she settled into what she knew would only be a temporary situation. When she bid goodbye to the children at the end of the year, it was with sadness.

The following year, 1935, she was hired to teach school at Tusas, which meant she could live at home. Oh, joy!

Every morning she walked a mile and a half to the little log building where she did her own janitor work. She left home at 7:30 so she could start a fire and the building would be warm by 9 o'clock. Twelve to fifteen children were enrolled. It was necessary that she keep a daily attendance of ten on the average. At times, she barely made that quota. There was only one Anglo family, the rest were Mexican, some of whom spoke very little English. They learned quickly by playing games such as jacks.

They drank river water, but they had real desks with inkwells in them, and at the front of the class were displayed the American flag and the New Mexico state flag.

A minor election was coming up, but she had no serious thoughts on politics. Party was a family thing. After years of listening to her father, a staunch Democrat, and Old Man Patchen, a vicious Republican, argue politics, it would be only natural for her to vote Democrat. Big mistake. She was about to be initiated into New Mexico politics.

Her boss teacher, who was a Patchen, told her to sign up as an independent, then puffed up her bosom and peered at her like an old owl. "That is, if you want to continue teaching in New Mexico."

Filled with indignation, Edna consulted Pop on the subject that weekend at the ranch.

He was only too happy to educate her, being one of those "upstart Democrats" who had caused so much trouble the past few years.

Relaxed in his favorite chair, he explained: "Since the railroad days of the 1880s until the early twenties, this town was ruled by a Republican ex-lawyer, Edwin Seward. At one time he was in tight with the land grant grabbers. By the time the McCowans came to Tres Piedras, the poor man was getting old and losing his grip. And wouldn't you know these new store owners turned out to be vicious Democrat upstarts. It's taken nearly five years but the newcomers are about to win." Pop's eyes took on a definite gleam.

"My boss said that the county superintendent can hire or fire me if I don't agree with his politics." Edna shifted uncomfortably.

"I expect that may still be true, but things are finally changing. These old line Republicans are shocked that anyone would dare to oppose them. They've been dictating to the Mexican mountain people for fifty years. But our time is coming. You just watch. The Democrats are fixing to take over New Mexico."

Teaching at the tiny log school in Tusas didn't last either. Edna began to wonder if she would ever get to stay in one place for more than a year. Oh, well as long as she remained close enough to home to get back when she got too homesick, teaching would have to do. And there was always the dances and parties.

The following fall, she went to teach in Red River, still not too far from home, but not nearly as close as Tusas or Taos Junction. Still she saw the old gang regularly. Aunt Bonnie and Uncle Perk had moved to Tres Piedras the previous year and still attended dances.

Having registered as an independent didn't work out too well for Edna in Red River, but she learned they couldn't fire her for her politics. Thank goodness.

She boarded with a family named Munden. They owned the first tourist cabin site there. The cabins weren't used in the winter, and staying there was the only memorable experience she came away with. They treated her like part of the family.

She remained there for two years, the first time that had happened in the town in ten years. Understandable. Other than leaving her happy relationship with the Mundens, she was glad to leave. Politics ran rampant in the town that was split down the middle. This made for plenty of arguments and dissent.

Diary Entry—1936

This summer I spent a couple of weeks with the Cooneys in North Dakota. Immersing myself once more in that Victorian life reminded me just how strict Grandmother Cooney is. And the aunts as well. Still, I will always be grateful to all of them for taking in that scared and lonely nine-year-old girl who believed her father was dying. And keeping me close in those years that were so important to my growing up, and when I was so vulnerable. Aunt Sarah and Aunt Rose will live forever in my heart, and every child in the world should have an Aunt Alice in their lives.

At twelve I escaped, but their influence will always affect the way I live. While I was there this summer I went to Fargo wearing jeans, just to make sure that I was my own person and not theirs. And horror of horrors, I smoked a cigarette in public in Sheldon. That naughty rebellion was something I had to get out of my system.

Edna returned home from North Dakota to find her own family in transition. Pop had bought a farm far from Tusas where he planned to raise more potatoes. The move would change their lives as nothing else ever had.

Though she had taught in several schools and boarded with friends and strangers, she could not let go the ranch life she loved so much. Clearly, no matter what else she did, she would be tied to it forever. If Pop sold Tusas it would break her heart.

"You aren't selling Tusas, are you?" She paused in packing what belongings they would take to Puncha Valley, fearful of his answer.

He stopped what he was doing. "No, whatever made you ask that? This is our home, always will be. One day you'll marry, and I want this for you." He put an arm around her. "I know how much you love this place. I'd never sell it."

The lump in her throat melted and she turned from him so he wouldn't see the tears in her eyes.

"You know what I'd like," he said, and she could tell by the gruffness in his voice he fought tears himself.

"No, what?"

"Let's go for a ride."

She looked around the cluttered room. At the boxes, more of them empty than packed, at stacks of belongings. "Now?"

"Why not? This'll be here when we get back. I'll go tell Mom."

"She'll have a wall-eyed fit."

He grinned. "I know, but her wall-eyed fits aren't so bad, are they?"

"No. They're not."

"Meet you in the barn."

She fitted a stack of Zane Grey pulp magazines into one corner of an empty box and went to her room to change.

As it turned out, he was waiting for her when she stepped into the cool, dark interior that smelled of hay and leather and horses.

"You want to fetch the horses?" he asked, taking two bridles off the wall.

"Sure." She went out back and scanned the pastures, then spotted the small herd. They grazed in long shadows cast by a triangular patch of juniper along the rim of a draw. The sun hung low in the sky, a breeze kissed her cheeks, carrying the fragrance of sage blossoms.

Before she was halfway to them, they spotted her and pricked their ears to gaze in curious expectation. Much as she liked them all, she still missed Tony. How foolish it had been to sell a horse she loved just so she could belong to a life she no longer cared about. But perhaps that, like many other life's lessons, was valuable.

"Come on over here, you guys," she shouted, and they pretended ignorance for a moment, gazing in all directions as if they saw something more important.

Finally, Old Bill ambled her way. He'd grown gray around the muzzle and eyes, but he still liked a good ride through the countryside. She'd take him, leave Pop's favorite, Buck, for him. The others followed, and the mules, Jake and Jack, came too. Where there were humans, there was a chance of something good to eat. She'd give them all a measure of grain when she and Pop came back.

Pop and Buck led the way circling around fields green with row after row of young potato plants, their treasures tucked firmly beneath the soil.

For a while they played "remember when," each choosing their favorite memory. It surprised her that one of Pop's was the week he took her on roundup and how he had delighted in dragging her out of bed each morning. And blushing, he admitted to deliberately overworking her to set her on another path. "I didn't think it should be your legacy to do ranch work all your life."

She fell silent for long moments, then told him her best memory.

"I remember when I was twelve and Mom came to North Dakota to bring me home. And the minute I laid eyes on this place again. Up till then, I'd been a kid...I mean a real kid. But that day, I knew deep down that I was going to live here forever...spend all my life on this place."

"Grown up, huh?" Pop said, chuckling.

"Well, I know...but yes, in certain ways. You know, when you first realize that life isn't just today or tomorrow, but for always, and it's not just you that's important, but everyone. And one day you'll be old? That kind of grown up."

He didn't laugh anymore, but swung to one side in his saddle and studied her closely for a moment.

Old Bill snorted and tossed his head away from a chamisa shrub blowing in the wind. She patted his neck. "Don't be silly, old fella. It's only rabbit brush. He's getting spooky in his old age."

"Some of us get that way," Pop said.

Fear skittered through her and was gone, as quick as a prairie dog popping into his hole. "You're not old."

"Older than I was once."

They never talked about his illness, the disease everyone said never left but hung around to strike again when it was least expected. Sometimes she forgot it for days at a time. Then something would remind her that a killer lurked within her father's body, and she would experience that fear she'd felt as a child when Mom took him away and left her behind. In spite of understanding why she had done it, Edna didn't think she'd ever quite forgive her mother, even though she loved her with all her heart.

This was something she could never tell her father, and she wondered why she thought of it now, when they were reminiscing about the best parts of their lives.

"You know, Pop, I really enjoyed herding the sheep that summer."

"Better than wrestling some old steer, wasn't it?"

"I think I liked it best because it was so quiet and peaceful and I could read and watch the colors of the desert and the mountains change as the sun moved across the sky."

"Well, if you liked it so much, why don't I let Pablo go and you can quit teaching and come home and herd sheep?"

They both had a good laugh, then she said, "Don't tempt me," and they were quiet.

He reined in Buck on a rise so they could look back down on the ranch house and outbuildings. "You aren't sorry, are you?"

"About what?"

"Well, I always thought your mom…we forced you into teaching, and you might have preferred something else."

"Well, sure I would. But you were right, you know. I can't make a living working the ranch with you. I have to earn my keep, and I sure didn't want to be a nurse. Not much else for a woman to do, is there? Even when I do settle on Tusas, there may be times I'll need to work. I could do a lot worse than teaching."

"So I guess all our choices have been for the best."

"So far they have, but I'm not sure about Puncha Valley. Why are we leaving here to go there?"

"Because there's not enough land here to support growing potatoes and livestock as well. Because I want to do one, and have to do the other to make a living. We'll manage to do both, with help. You'll see, it'll work out. We'll always have the land. Remember that."

Raising potatoes on such a large scale turned out to be hard work. In many ways harder than ranching.

They had three or four teams of work horses and each team required one man. During crop time there were from four to eight men to feed every day. There might have been help in the fields digging the crop, but in the house Mom had only Grams, and Edna when she was home. Even in the off season when she was away teaching, they kept from two to four boys on hand all the time, and they were a part of the family. That meant feeding, laundry, mending and cleaning up after all of them.

There were three two-bedroom apartments besides the main house. Grams and Gramps had one, and cousin Max, who had followed his dreams to New Mexico, and his wife, Katie Ford's daughter Thelma, who had followed their dream to New Mexico had another, and the third slept the hands. Edna would not be there much.

Mom called it a lonesome and forsaken place, and Edna agreed. Puncha Valley was probably the worst place to live Edna had ever seen. Seventeen miles out of town and no close neighbors. Its only redeeming quality was the unbroken close view of the breathtaking Sangre de Cristos.

Chapter Thirteen

Edna's Diary—Summer, 1937

Puncha Valley is indeed a remote place. I worry about Mom getting lonely, but she is kept very busy as the work is hard. I must continue with my plans to teach in these little mountain schools and take summer classes in teaching methods. One day, perhaps I'll finish college, but for now I want to remain here on the high desert. These tiny schools are so in need of teachers who care about the children. I fear it won't be too long before they are all gone. Already, the first school where I taught, Taos Junction, has been closed. The children are being bussed along with those from Carson and Servilleta to Ojo Caliente. And so I have applied for a teaching job there. They will hire two teachers.

* * *

In the early '30s, New Mexico had taken local school boards away from the schools and made a rule that the county superintendent would hire all the teachers. The local boards only responsibility was to maintain the school buildings. Edna was hired by the county superintendent to teach at Ojo Caliente for the 1937-38 school term for the princely sum of $65 a month.

There were two rooms and two teachers. High school was held elsewhere. She would teach fourth through eighth grades, twenty pupils. The first day at the school found her a bit nervous. Some of the students would be larger than her. Swinging the door open, she raised her chin, squared her shoulders and stepped into the room assigned to the upper grades.

Immediate quiet greeted her.

"Good morning." She strode to the front, just as if she knew precisely what she was doing, and introduced herself, picked up the enrollment sheet lying on her desk, and began to read, then smiled at a fond memory.

"I see there aren't any eighth graders, so I'm going to promote one of the seventh graders. I skipped a grade into eighth when I went to school in Tres Piedras, and I turned out just fine, so don't worry."

A chuckle and a bit of horseplay followed, but when she glanced over the room, everyone settled down.

"Jerry Archuleta, you are now in seventh-eighth grade. Hold up your hand, would you?"

A solemn, round-faced boy eased brown fingers into the air.

Everyone giggled.

She waited for them to quiet, then called the roll and got down to work. And these students knew how to work. When it came to play they were equally talented. In addition to regular studies, there was a swimming class, which was a delight to everyone.

Living in Ojo Caliente differed a lot from Taos Junction and Tusas. The popular hot springs was first used by the Indians, then the Spanish, but pretty much everyone used it now.

The Chili Line had never reached the small town that had grown up around the springs. Because of the sawmill and lumber industry Halleck & Howard had added a branch of the Chili Line to run from Taos Junction to La Madera. Passengers could ride, but they weren't catered to in any way.

A bus ran from Ojo Caliente to Taos via Taos Junction. The town was pretty well cut-off from through traffic. If someone was there, it was because they came intentionally, mostly for the hot springs cure. No one "passed through" on their way somewhere else like in the small towns that had sprung up along the Chili Line.

Edna soon got to know everyone, and this time there was no danger she would be lonely. Gram and Gramps would live with her. Compared to the climate at Ojo Caliente, Puncha Valley was bitterly cold, and they would be good company. She rented a two-room apartment in a large two-story house belonging to the Hernandez family, perhaps a little crowded, but she was gone all day. Besides Gram and Gramps were so easy to get along with. She felt as if the three of them were a family, same as they had been when she was small. Even when she did things they didn't approve of they never fussed.

One Saturday night she attended a dance with three local bachelors, Raymond Gentry, Dalford Stover and George Rogers, not the best-looking men in town by far, but they'd do for escorts. It wouldn't be proper for her to attend alone. Besides, she'd go with just about anyone if it meant getting to dance.

The next morning when she went in to breakfast, Gram was sitting in her little rocker. She peered at Edna from over her glasses and said, "Well, you couldn't have picked three uglier men in the whole country."

Gramps chuckled and said, "Maybe that's why they are still bachelors."

She laughed along with them.

They lived directly across from the Santa Cruz Church, which was in a flux. The villagers were having a difficult time deciding whether to renovate the old church or build a new one. Every Sunday morning the bell tolled for Mass, and she would lie in bed gazing out the window, watching the mourning doves flee the tower, marveling at how their silver wings caught the sunlight. Such breathtaking beauty God had wrought.

One Sunday she walked down to the springs, crossing the cattle guard that kept free range stock out. Five different minerals were said to be contained in the hot water that bubbled from the earth. It was also said that people who bathed and drank of the waters for twenty-one days would be cured, whatever their ailment. She looked forward to viewing that first-hand.

Then she hiked up the hill to one of the old Indian campsites where a handful of people dug in the dry red earth. The October sun was warm, the air dry and breezy. She watched for a while, chatted with one of the women who came into the shade to rest.

"What are they doing?" she asked the woman.

"Looking for pots to sell to tourists and collectors in Taos."

"Ah." Edna watched some more, then waved at the woman and continued her hike. There were six such campsites around the springs, and all were active. Must be a profitable endeavor, this selling of pots.

She had only been there a couple of weeks when she heard of dances held up on the hill behind the Bluebird Café and Terecita's Restaurant. A jukebox provided the music. She was glad, for she missed the dances at Tres Piedras that were held in an old barber shop building. The Martinez family furnished live music there, playing Spanish tunes on fiddles and guitars. Some of the dances were similar to the square dances, minus a caller. In no time, she became acquainted with a couple of young families who regularly drove over to Tres Piedras, and so she started going with them when there were no dances in Ojo Caliente.

Distance was no obstacle, provided someone had a wagon or car, especially if everyone had a good time.

One Monday morning, arriving silently in class, she overheard her first-ever story of brujas. Her talent for eavesdropping came in handy, as the children weren't always eager to talk in front of adults. So she remained quiet and listened.

"My uncle, he was coming home last night and he saw lights…it was the bruja," one of the boys said.

Wide-eyed, the children oohed and aahed.

The fifth-grader nodded. "He told me if I'm not good the bruja will get me."

Well, what works, works, Edna thought, but said nothing about hearing the tale. If it took the fear of a bruja to make the students so well-behaved, then who was she to question it?

The villagers in favor of restoring the old Santa Cruz Church finally lost the battle, but managed to prevent it being torn down. Soon, they built the new St. Mary's Church, but, to their dismay, when they went to move the bell from Santa Cruz, they found someone had taken it.

After that, she missed the ringing of the bell every Sunday morning.

The following year, she completed a circle in her life and went to Tres Piedras to teach. As she walked up the steps to the porch, she felt much as she had when she'd gone to school there. A little fear, a lot of excitement.

She'd first seen the Tres Piedras school house in 1922, long before starting to school there. Back in 1920 Mr. Seward had decided that Tres Piedras had outgrown its two-room school. In need of more votes to be reelected, he shook up the Taos County school board and they planned this beautiful four-room school with a basement for a central heating system. But they ran out of money and only one corner of the basement was finished.

Oh, but how she remembered the beautiful white plastered school with its sky-blue trim. The building smelled so new, piney and painty. And everyone loved it.

Right away, Mrs. Perkins and some other ladies were invited to a get-together in the new but unfinished school for a demonstration on how to make purses out of discarded inner tubes. It was a first step in recycling. The purses were very pretty with a handle and inner lining with pockets. But they smelled so bad.

What Edna remembered best was the fun she and her best friend Lena Jo had exploring upstairs and downstairs of the new Tres Piedras school and how they created stories of adventures that could take place in such a huge building. Later she would go to school there, and be passed up from seventh to eighth grade.

Now, here she was, teaching at Tres Piedras and boarding with the McCowans. And going to dances every Saturday night, once more fussing with Calvin Hiller over everything but the jukebox selections.

Some of her students liked to bring pinon nuts to school. The secret was keeping the teacher from catching them. It was a matter of learning how to crack and peel them with teeth and tongue and spitting out the shells without getting caught.

Whenever there was a good year, pinons were shipped out by the carload on the train. The crop was unpredictable. Some areas produced every three years, some at five years and some at seven. They brought from 7 to 12 cents a pound.

As it turned out, her first year at Tres Piedras proved to be a good year for pinons. What a task keeping the eating and spitting under control. Most of the kids were really good at not getting caught. But there were more disturbing matters to deal with than kids spitting pinon shells.

Like the noisy construction going on around them, for this year was the year the school board decided to reconstruct the building. They designed a gymnasium out of the two west rooms. They finished digging out the basement so that the ceiling would be high enough to accommodate basketball games. This went on for the solid nine months she taught there.

During that time election day came around, and she and Pop had a good time discussing and anticipating the upcoming festivities.

Sitting around the supper table the weekend before the big day, Pop grinned real wide. "This election day is going to be something to watch."

Indeed, it was. By daylight Florida McCowan was up and rattling around in the boarding house kitchen cooking up a storm. By seven she was out of the house and in her little Model-T truck, chugging the engine noisy in the still morning. Off Florida would go to fetch the first of the voters. After a while she returned, the truck crammed with as many folks as she could stuff in the seat and bed. They'd no more than pile out then she was off for another load. Sometimes she'd drive as far as ten miles. Then she would feed them all their lunch and make a second round. They must have appreciated the ride and lunch, because most of them voted Democrat. No one would be left out. If they didn't understand the system, she could show them.

It wasn't quite like the old days, but close. Back then the landed families were the patrons who could tell the people who lived and worked on their places how to vote.

Florida didn't go quite that far, but her actions certainly influenced the voters. She was quite an individual. She had one God and that was money. You couldn't talk to her five minutes without her bringing it into the conversation in some way.

When Edna was younger she remembered her mother taking Florida's son to the ranch for a week or two at a time. In return Edna would stay with Florida. She was old enough to work and help as a stocker in the store and in the boarding house which Florida also ran. Though much younger, Edna had never been able to keep up with the hard-working Florida and soon gave up trying.

This election morning, even as the voters lined up to put their marks on the ballot, fistfights broke out in the dusty yard. Everyone crowded around cheering and shouting. Once the two fighters wore out, they'd all get back in line, as if nothing much had happened. Until someone else disagreed, then the fist-a-cuffs would start all over again. Pop had been right. Election day was indeed exciting.

For nearly ten years a dispute had raged over putting the highway west across the river. All that time the ruling faction in Santa Fe was mostly Republicans. But at last the Democrats came into power, and the highway was started west of the Rio Grande Gorge.

The McCowans had built a big new store and house in town. Now they built a dance hall and restaurant. The hall was big enough to hold basketball games. Those upstart Democrats were making things happen, just as Pop had predicted.

Mom wasn't at the ranch the next weekend when Edna visited.

"She's off nursing some young fellow," Pop explained. "Folks came out from Oklahoma, man and his wife and three sons. They seem to be pretty well off. Plenty of nice things."

"What's wrong with him?"

"They said it was typhoid. Mom is apt to be there a while."

"You sound worried."

Pop threaded his fingers together over his stomach and leaned back in the chair. "Not really, but this boy is eighteen and your Mom is leery of taking care of a boy that age on her own."

It was six weeks before Mom came home, with quite a tale to tell. The boy had pulled through.

Edna helped her set the table the Sunday after she returned, eager to hear her story.

"I don't think the mother is all there."

"You mean she's crazy?"

"Well, not exactly, just slow."

Mom took a roast from the oven and carried it to the table. "She can't cook. All the time I was there we ate boiled potatoes, boiled turnips and boiled beef twice a day. Can you imagine?"

Mom did the doctoring, but Doc Martin sent one of the other doctors in Taos out about every two weeks to check on everything and prescribe medicines. Doc Martin never came across the river.

The story made Edna doubly glad she'd decided to teach instead of becoming a nurse. Not that the decision had been hers, but it worked out, nevertheless.

That winter was bitterly cold and snow fell day and night until the only way to get around was by sled.

The phone rang one evening and Edna answered.

"Hi, it's Imogene Patchen. How are you?"

"We're fine, and you?"

"The same. Listen, we've been invited to attend the grand opening of the Sage Brush Inn in Taos. You know the one Tony Lujan and Mabel Dodge built...or are still building?"

"Oh, my. That's exciting. Are you going?"

"Of course, and we want you to go with us."

Edna caught her breath, unable to answer for a moment.

"You there? Did you hear me?"

"Yes...yes. Wow, that would be super. Are you sure it's all right?"

"Oh, yes, they said we should bring guests. It's a huge affair, and you'll want to dress up."

Mabel Dodge and Antonio Lujan were the best party givers in New Mexico. Writers and artists, famous people like Thornton Wilder, Thomas Wolfe, Aldous Huxley, Carl Jung, Edward Hopper and Mary Austin often dropped by. Once Mabel Dodge had a dinner party for the writer, D.H. Lawrence. It was said she hoped he would write a book about her. So far that hadn't happened.

Antonio Lujan had been Mabel's chauffeur, but eventually she had married him, even though he already had an Indian wife by the name of Candelaria. He himself was a Tewa Indian, and Mabel immediately embraced his culture.

Edna hung up the phone and danced around the room. Once she settled down enough to explain, Pop said, "I guess we'll have to figure out a way to get you to such a splendid affair. Wouldn't want you to miss it."

Outside, the snow had piled up so deep that the Chevrolet couldn't plow through it.

"What will you wear?" Mom asked.

"The emerald green transparent velvet dress I bought in Albuquerque last summer. It cost me ten dollars. You remember, I showed it to you and you asked where I ever thought I'd wear that. Certainly not to a Saturday night dance in Tres Piedras."

Mom nodded, a frown creasing her forehead. "Well, I don't know how you're going to get there."

Edna knew Mother would like to be going to the party as well, and felt bad that she wasn't.

Pop, who'd gone back to reading Zane Grey, glanced up, marking his place with a finger.

"I gave Tom Lowance a milk cow for part of his wages. He's been wanting to get it home. We can load Edna and that cow onto the sled. The mules can pull it and take them into Tres Piedras. Tom will get his cow and she can go to her party."

Excitement building, Edna pirouetted. "I'll call Florida and make sure I can stay there overnight so I can catch the train to the Patchens' house in Taos Junction the next morning. Oh, Pop, thank you. Thank you."

She threw her arms around her surprised father, then circled around the room once again. Everyone would be dancing. What a wonderful time she would have. And no telling who she might get to meet. Mabel Dodge and Tony Lujan. Wow.

Once safely delivered to Tres Piedras on the sled, along with Tom Luance's cow, Edna spent the night with Florida and rode the train over to Taos Junction. From there she traveled with the Patchens by car to Taos.

The Sage Brush Inn had been built about halfway between Taos and Ranchos de Taos. There was a huge crowd at the grand opening. People from Santa Fe to Questa came. They bought their supper there and then there was a dance with live music. Oh, it was a great affair, and she could hardly believe she was there.

Dance after dance, she went from one man's arms into another's, whirling under the twinkling lights, scarcely pausing between sets.

Tony and Mabel Lujan took the crowd on a tour of all the finished rooms of the rambling abode. Edna was fascinated with Mabel, who as a white woman, had adopted the Pueblo way of dressing. She wore her thick chestnut hair as they did, with bangs covering her forehead to frame wide gray eyes. The couple appeared devoted, though it was an odd pairing. Mabel had all the money, but Tony appeared well-to-do and comfortable around her friends.

Edna returned eagerly to the dance floor after the tour, dancing on into the night.

Leaving a partner, she glanced over the crowd and saw the Patchens motioning to her. They were ready to leave. She took a step and came face to face with Antonio Lujan himself. Over six feet tall and adorned in colorful Pueblo attire, he wore his ebony hair in two plaits. She felt so tiny standing before him. Shivers ran down her back and she just kept smiling up at him like an idiot. Such a handsome man.

Say something. Anything.

She tried, but she couldn't.

Then he did. "Might I have this dance?"

He held out a hand, large and broad and brown.

She swallowed, dragged in a deep breath. "Oh, I'm sorry," she said, unable to recognize her own shaky voice. "But we were just leaving. Thank you. I…thank…"

With that she whirled away from him and shoved her way through the crowded dancers.

She approached John and Imogene Patchen and knew her face was flushed red. "Oh, dear. Oh, my goodness."

"What in the world is wrong?" John asked. "Are you all right? Did someone—?"

"No, nothing like that. I can't believe I did that. I can't believe he—"

"Child, stop babbling. What is it?"

"Tony Lujan...he asked me for a dance."

"He did. That's wonderful," Imogene said, "...isn't it?"

"Well, yes, of course, but I...I can't believe I told him no."

"You didn't. What were you thinking?"

"I guess I wasn't. He's so...large...and imposing...and he's married to Mable Dodge."

"Yes, so?"

John, who had stood by in gruff silence, said, "Well, come on, let's go. And Edna, I'm going to make you walk the canyon. Tony owes me fifteen dollars and he thought you were one of the Patchens. Now I'll never get it."

Chapter Fourteen

Edna's Diary—July, 1940

In a week I will become Mrs. Calvin Hiller. We will marry in Taos. Thinking back on it, I can't quite comprehend that I ever disliked this man who is gentle as a kitten and hard as nails. His brother Dago taught him to use his fists when he was small and he learned to be a fighter, but he has a great sense of humor. He was also an excellent basketball player in high school. And he's so big and strong. Five years of being around each other plus our mutual love of swing music finally brought us together.

Falling in love is a strange condition. I remember the first time I ever saw him, this big bouncer who never went near the dance floor. I thought he was just too funny, he spoke with a strong Kentucky drawl. Looking back on it, I'm still amazed we ever got together.

Tres Piedras—1935

Bonnie and Perk no longer needed to chaperone Edna, for she had turned twenty-one that summer. The Perkins had moved from the cabin on the ranch to Tres Piedras. All being dancing fools, it was natural they would continue to go to the McCowans' house to dance on Saturday nights.

And the first person Edna saw as the men surrounded her to get on her dance card, was the big, tall bouncer engaged in conversation with Mr. McCowan. He had a thatch of blond hair and broad shoulders, and stood way out from the crowd. She'd never seen him before. He must have sensed her staring, for he glanced in her

170

direction, then away like maybe she'd thrown a rock at him. Mr. McCowan peered at her a moment, so she guessed the guy had asked him about her.

Well, he needn't bother. She dragged her attention back to filling in her dance card. There were never enough girls to go around at the dances, so she didn't have to worry about being a wallflower. She sure wasn't interested in anyone who didn't dance.

Swinging around the floor to a waltz tune, she and her partner passed nearby where Calvin stood talking to Florida in his thick Kentucky drawl. Another strike against him. And if he didn't get out on the dance floor soon, that would be strike three. A man who didn't dance was just plain unnatural.

She'd have to find out who he was.

"Why that's our nephew, Calvin's sister's boy," Florida McCowan told her when she casually mentioned the stranger. "His name is Calvin, too. Named after his uncle. He's come to stay with us a while, and because of his size, Calvin thought he would be a good bouncer. Keep the riff-raff from beating each other to a pulp. Why, dear? Would you like me to introduce you to him?"

"No, of course not. I was just curious."

"Uh-hum." Florida rolled her eyes.

"I'm not interested in any man. Romance is the farthest thing from my mind. Get all involved with a man, and the good times are gone. I just want to have fun, but right away a man wants you to do what he likes, doesn't want to do what you like. I'm footloose and fancy free, and I intend to stay that way." She glanced toward the bouncer. "How long is he going to be here?"

Florida laughed. "Why, honey, I think he's here to stay."

The rest of that summer flew by and she did her best to pay little attention to Calvin Hiller. He was there, that was all. And she certainly had plenty of men asking her to dance so she didn't have to pay any mind to a tall, rawboned Kentucky fellow.

Over time they continued to run into each other, and she began to think he arranged the meetings. He started showing up at dances in Taos Junction.

Seeing him hanging around watching and not doing much of anything else, she approached him between sets.

"Did they hire you as a bouncer here too?"

"Nah. I like the music."

"Dance music?"

"Listening music." A wide grin lit up his eyes.

"You're impossible."

"And you're stuck up."

"Well, if that's your opinion why do you keep hanging around everywhere I go?"

"Stuck on yourself, aren't you? What makes you think I come to see you?"

She swept her glance around the room. "Oh, I don't know. Why else would you be here?"

"I told you, to listen to the music."

"You could do that at Florida's. She has a jukebox."

He nodded, said nothing, just looked down at her for a long time, then shrugged and walked off.

And so things went, until the fall of 1939 when she got a job teaching in Tres Piedras and boarded with Florida McCowan. There was no avoiding Calvin.

"Okay, everyone ante up a nickel and we'll play the jukebox," Calvin said, just like he had every evening since she'd come to stay at the boarding house.

And just as she always did, Edna asked for swing music.

"My favorite, too," he said, like he always did.

"Don't you like any other kind of music?" she asked.

"Well, some, but swing's my favorite."

"Funny, it's mine too."

His fingers brushed hers and held on for a minute when he took her nickel. She gave him a long look which he returned.

All during supper she caught him looking at her, but each time she did, he would get real busy doing something else, passing the bread, or talking to his aunt or uncle or one of the other boarders.

That year there were plenty of boarders sitting at Florida McCowan's table. The road crew building Highway 285 from Santa

Fe to the state line were all staying there, about twelve regulars, plus Calvin and Edna.

Her cousin Max was tall and gangly, and five years her junior. He had the soft drawl of all her kin who lived in Arkansas and was ornery as could be.

Katie Ford and Maggie Franklin were cooks and waitresses for the McCowans.

The Fords had a tall, pretty daughter named Thelma and she and Max took up with each other real quick. Sometimes the joking went on all evening between the younger of the group gathered at Florida's.

"You don't look like you eat very well," Calvin told Max.

Max eyed Calvin, grinned his big lopsided grin and said, "Bet I'd eat stuff you wouldn't even touch."

"Shoot, I'd eat anything that didn't move on my plate, even a porcupine," Calvin said, and glanced toward Edna, egging her on to saying something.

"I'd try a porcupine, I suppose, long as they took off the hide and quills," she replied.

"Me, too," said the shy Thelma.

Maggie Franklin hooted at them. "I'm gonna take you kids up on that. You're all invited to come to my house to eat porcupine."

After much laughter and discussion, eight of the younger set agreed, and a date was set for what would become the infamous porcupine supper.

When the time came Max took Thelma and Edna and drove out to the Franklins' house for supper.

Maggie's husband opened the door and ushered them in as more of the gang arrived. The house smelled wonderful, with scents of good food.

"Mmm, well porcupine smells good anyway," Max said.

"Well, that may be the roast beef. I convinced my wife she'd better cook something else in case you all backed out of partaking of our little de-quilled friend."

At last, with everyone seated at the table amid plenty of dares and joshing, the platter of porcupine meat was passed around. Max took a good portion, rubbed his belly and grinned. Calvin, not to be outdone, did the same. He handed the platter to Edna with an evil gleam in his eyes.

She lifted a chunk of the pale meat onto her plate, added portions of potatoes, vegetables and bread and butter. Calvin was watching her when she cut off a small bite and lifted the fork to her mouth.

"Well?" she taunted him. "Aren't you going to join me?"

"Uh, well, sure." He cut a piece and eyed it on his fork.

"You first," she said, laughing.

"Together, on three," he said.

Max hooted and put a bite in his mouth, chewing and making a horrible face before he swallowed. "Not bad," he said. "You two better get busy or I'm gonna win this contest." With that he took another bite.

Edna put hers to her lips; Calvin did to.

"On three," Max taunted and began to count.

At three both opened their mouths and took their first bite of porcupine.

It was not much different in taste from pork, just a little gamey. Edna wallowed it around on her tongue just in case they'd missed a quill or two.

After an evening of fun with everyone, time came to go home. As she put on her sweater, Calvin stood at her elbow.

"You know, you were such a good sport about this, I'd like to take you home."

Her heart did a little pitter-pat and she took the arm he offered. On the way back to Florida's, she found she didn't mind his Kentucky drawl at all; in fact she rather liked it.

He must have liked her too, even though he had called her stuck up, because he soon called her for a real date. One that almost got both of them killed.

Dad had made a down payment on a car for her with the warning she was not to let anyone else drive. This was 1939, and not many had a car, so he thought this was important. Calvin also had a car, and a reputation for being a fast driver. He'd had a couple of little wrecks, nothing serious.

Near Christmas of that year, the owner of the Madrid Coal Mines put up a huge Christmas light display. Everyone in the state was excited about it. He'd brought the idea back from Pennsylvania.

A trip to see the lights would be their biggest date, but when they went out to get in the car, Calvin turned on the key, punched at the starter and nothing happened. He tried again. Still no response.

Edna sat there watching him, thinking how badly she wanted to see the lights.

He climbed out and lifted the hood and fiddled around under there a while. "I think the battery's dead." He came to her window. "I'm so sorry. I know how much you wanted to see the lights."

"We can take my car," she said.

"No, no. that wouldn't be right. Taking your car on a date? No, I couldn't let you do that."

"Yes, please, Calvin. I don't want to miss the lights. I'm not supposed to let anyone drive my car, so I'd have to drive. It'll be okay."

"What if somebody sees us?"

"Don't be silly. Who would care?"

"I would. It's not manly."

"Well, what if I said I'll just take my car and go alone? Then what would you say?"

He sat there a long time, staring out the window. Then, softly, "I couldn't let you do that."

She reached over and opened her door. "Well, then, let's go."

They hurried to her car, hopped in and took off. At Santa Fe, they ate at the Waffle House. When they came out into the brisk night air, she experienced the strangest feeling. One that told her something bad was going to happen if she got behind the wheel. Having had a few premonitions in her life, she thought about it for a moment, then handed Calvin the keys.

"I think you'd better drive."

"Are you sure? What'll your dad say?"

"I don't know, I just don't want to drive tonight."

They weren't even out of town good, chatting and laughing, when a car sideswiped another car, sending it barreling straight for them.

All she could remember was watching with horror as the headlights bore down on them, Calvin jerking the wheel to get them out of the way. The car smashed into the rear fender of her car. He'd avoided a head-on by mere inches.

For a few minutes, she sat still, eyes squeezed shut, shaking so hard she couldn't speak.

During that time all she knew was his big hand on her arm, his voice saying, "Are you all right? Are you hurt?" and him touching her to see if she was bleeding or broken.

Then he gathered her into his arms so she could cry in relief that they had been spared.

"Come on, let's get out."

He had to slide across and get out on her side because his door wouldn't open.

A car coming down the road stopped.

"You kids okay?" someone yelled out the window.

Calvin waved. "Yes, we're fine."

"We'll stop in Santa Fe and call the police and a wrecker," the man offered.

"That would be good. Thanks so much," Calvin said, then keeping his arm around her waist, he supported her to a place where they could sit and wait.

Another car behind them had also been struck by the careening car, and its passengers came to sit beside them. No one was seriously injured, but they had to wait over two hours before everything was taken care of.

When she told the woman from the other car goodbye, she took her hand and squeezed it.

"You are lucky to be with such a fine young man."

"Yes. Yes, I am," Edna replied.

And that was what he was to her from then on.

In April, Calvin said he had plans to go to Cincinnati or Detroit to look for a "war job" since things were picking up and the Depression was almost over.

Then he sat, pulled her down beside him, looked her in the eye and said, "When are we going to get married?"

She looked right back at him, and remarked jokingly, "Oh, about the first Friday after the first Tuesday in July."

He took her seriously, and they were married in Taos on that exact date in 1940, with plans to go east in September. That would never be, for the first draft was set and he volunteered. He lacked two weeks of serving his one-year service when Pearl Harbor was attacked. The next time she saw him he was in a hospital in Brigham City, Utah. And their lives would never be the same again.

Epilogue

On my 85th birthday, Bonnie and Perk's boy Jim, who has been a treasure to me all these years, took me for what I knew would be my final horseback ride. We rode all over the hills around Tusas. I felt as if I were bidding my life goodbye. But that's fine. My God has watched over me and taken good care of me. He holds my hand. I sometimes wonder why doesn't he let me go.

Until recently, I spent a lot of time traveling between the ranch, abandoned now except for roundups, and I see places that bring back fond memories.

That bright pink building in Tres Piedras that now houses crafts was once the school where I taught. It was around 1945, with the war over and some money available that the building was finally repaired. It was then the bright pink paint appeared, probably the only color they could lay hands on. And the building remains pink to this day, though it hasn't been a school in a long, long time. Tres Piedras has had no school for many years.

Edna's Journal—1990

The year is rapidly spinning away. Someday when I get big, I am going to buy a big rock on the coast of the Pacific, or maybe Cabo San Lucas, where I can sit and listen to the surf hour after hour. Or maybe I'll settle for a fast-moving stream and falls. Or maybe perfect stillness at a perfect sunset. Now where shall I put the sunset? Over Tusas peaks? A North Dakota prairie? Into the Pacific? Over a snow-filled San Luis valley?

Sunset and the evening star. I like to think of stars as those who have gone before. They give me a warm feeling of those watching over me as I will watch when my time comes with that one clear call for me.

There's Calvin, that bright one yonder. He twinkles a lot. I know his pain is gone. And we had a good life. Two darling girls completed our family. His strength and wonderful sense of humor probably carried him through 22 years of pain that tied him to a wheelchair after the war took his legs. He fought long and hard, but I lost him in 1967. I never remarried, for no other man could ever suit me.

We had bought the Sewell place on the Tusas below Dad's. And that is where I go when I long to visit the past.

And that small star nearby Calvin's. That's our firstborn, our sweet Annie. She lost her own battle with death after becoming a wife and mother. I smile remembering the way Mom insisted on being in the labor room when she was born. Making sure everything went all right. And how she insisted on naming our little doll Catherine Ann, after her. Mom became as much a mother to her as I was. I always joked with Mom that if she didn't have someone to take care of she wasn't happy. I believe she was more of a mother than I ever was.

She's that star looking over Annie's shoulder, making sure she's all right even today. We lost Mom in 1973, Pop and I. As is often the case, Pop's caregiver wore out before her patient. Pop was a gentle, soft-spoken man who made friends slowly, but those he made he kept. Pop, who fought TB to a standstill back in the days when that wasn't easy...well, he's up there too, following Mom three years later and twinkling at her side in the night sky.

My God is really close to me, but not always found in church. I find him in the perfection of color and design of a flower, a blazing sunrise, a baby's smile, the rocks and colors of the Moab country. A starry, snowy night, a good friend's understanding, and in certain music, the ocean surf and on and on.

Churches, yes, I have felt him in a little church in Puerta Penasco, where the members had no benches, but knelt on the floor. In the little log school house where we used to go to sing the old songs and spend the day in good fellowship. In the little Catholic church in North Dakota, the incense, the Latin service, in the tabernacle in Salt Lake City, the music there.

I have searched many places to find a church I could belong to, but always something stops me. I must keep going for I admire deeply all those who can give themselves to one belief saying this is it. This is mine. I try only to live by the Golden Rule: Do unto others, and the Indian motto: Don't judge others until you have walked in their moccasins. So my God dwells within me, not Catholic, Presbyterian or Buddhist, but in my soul.

It doesn't matter where I go or what I do or what is done to me, I can derive peace and happiness from the smell of sage, the quiet of a pinon forest, the beauty of the blue balled juniper. In the laughter of my grandchildren, both Annie's and Linda's.

Ah, my Linda. Pop bought a ranch in Antonito, Colorado, in 1945, where he could raise feed crops and graze the cattle during the winter. Linda and her husband Pat run that ranch, but I still keep my nose in things. So I have the ranches, and my lovely daughter and son-in-law and my grandchildren.

And so long as we have glorious sunsets and God gives us a new day, make the best of it. Why look in the gutter when stars are overhead?

All my life has been packed away in little boxes.

My dad came home from the hospital. He gave me a wooden box he had made in therapy. I was twelve and my box went with me wherever I went. I lost the bracelet, my friends changed to lovers, my gloves wore and were discarded, as were the lovers, who were replaced by my husband.

His letters from war fields then filled that box. Other big boxes were acquired to hold all the things that make a home, wedding presents packed away for five years; on his return letters were replaced by the little box of keepsakes made by two precious little girls.

The big boxes served a busy in and out storage life for twenty years. Then a bigger box claimed life and all that was left were papers in safety deposit boxes. Memorial books and cards to be put in small boxes to be kept in the big storage boxes that contained all that was left of a home.

The little wooden box still goes with me—treasures may change, the box is solid like the ties of my family.

LaVergne, TN USA
17 August 2009
155048LV00002B/204/A